# Baba Bulleh Shah

## A Personal Interpretation

Dr. Wasim Ahmed

KHALIS HOUSE
PUBLISHING
FADED IN PRINT, LEGACY IN INK

ISBN 978-1-917021-13-5

Printed in the United Kingdom by KhalisHouse Publishing

www.KhalisHouse.com
info@KhalisHouse.com

Find us on:
Instagram/KhalisHouse

Dedicated to the loving memory of Sheena Whiteley.

# Contents

## Acknowledgments

I would like to acknowledge the help and support given by Ian Doyle, throughout the preparation of this book. I am extremely grateful for his helpful suggestions, editing and proof-reading of the manuscript.

I would also like to thank Ranveer Singh of Khalis House Publishing, for recognising the importance of Baba Bulleh Shah's poetry to the Punjabi heritage, and his kind support in making this book a reality.

# Introduction.

When I published my first book, 'Baba Bulleh Shah, A Selection of His Punjabi Poetry', my goal was to try and provide an accurate and modern translation of some of his most popular poetry. The aim was to help preserve his poetry by translating it into English, as the already available translations appeared to be either inadequate or contained errors in the way the original poetry was written and subsequently translated. The book was aimed at the new generation of Punjabi-speaking diaspora, mainly in the West, who are now searching for their own heritage, many having lost their ability to read, write or even speak their own mother-tongues. Hence in the book, I included English translations of forty of Baba Bulleh Shah's most famous poems, together with the poetry in the original Shahmukhi and Gurmukhi Punjabi texts. I also included transliteration of the original poetry for those who are unable to read or write Punjabi. This would help them understand the rhythmic musicality of this style of poetry, which is traditionally sung in the form of *qawwalis*, rather than recited.

While compiling my first book, I mainly focussed on translating the original text into English as closely as possible. What became apparent to me immediately was that translating such multifaceted Sufi poetry is nothing like translating a work of fiction or a set of instructions but is immensely complex. The word-play in Sufi poetry is both precise and diverse at the same time, and each word, line and verse can have multiple nuances and convey a plethora of meanings. What I have realised is that translation into English alone does not make the verse any more understandable, unless one is aware of the context and thinking behind it.

Looking at it another way. If we imagine reading a play by Shakespeare, though written in English, most people nowadays will struggle to understand what is being said or what historical event is being portrayed, unless notes accompanied the text explaining these. The language spoken then and now is English, but it has changed so much that much of it is difficult to follow for many people. The same applies to Punjabi literature from 300 years ago; it requires explanation of words, context and terms used in everyday language then, that are no longer familiar to us.

It is hard to imagine how different lifestyle would have been in the Punjab 300 years ago when people lived a much simpler life, mainly in the countryside. Since then, major upheavals have affected the region, culminating in an arbitrary division of the province by the retreating British Colonial Empire in 1947. This resulted in the larger Western Punjab forming the biggest province of Pakistan and Eastern Punjab became part of India.

The artificial lines drawn on a map by the Colonial British rendered this once united land into two, much like the banks of a river or tracks of a railway line, running towards their destination, separately but parallel to each other. The trauma of this violent division which may have resulted in up to a million deaths, is still fresh in peoples' minds. Instead of multiple Faiths living together, Western Punjab is now predominantly Muslim, and Eastern Punjab mainly Sikh. In this segregated style, with little contact between the two communities of Punjabis, people have forgotten knowledge of each other's customs, beliefs, lifestyles and even the shared Punjabi language has become divided.

The Punjabi language is an ancient tongue of this region and is still spoken by over 150 million people worldwide today. It was the greatest Sufi Saint of the Punjab, Baba Farid-ud-Din Ganjshaker (1173-1265), who first took up writing in his native Punjabi rather than Farsi (Persian), the lingua franca at the time. This tradition has been followed by subsequent Sufi Saints and poets.

Although the spoken Punjabi at the time was the same, it could be written in two different forms: Gurmukhi and Shahmukhi.

Gurmukhi uses characters from the indigenous tongues of the region and was formally organised by the second Sikh Guru, Guru Angad Dev Ji (1504-1552), whereas the Shahmukhi text used letters of the Arabic alphabet that were also used by the official Farsi language. Sufis like Baba Bulleh Shah would have written in both forms as there was no division in the Punjabi culture while the Punjab was united. During the Sikh Empire of Punjab and Kashmir, Gurmukhi Punjabi was the official version used, but it was not an issue for writers of all backgrounds who could read and write either script.

Since the forced division of the Punjab by the British Colonial powers however, the two halves have adopted their own versions so that in Western Punjab, Shahmukhi is written and in the Eastern half, Gurmukhi. After 75 years of separation, Punjabis from the two halves no longer understand these alternative versions of their own language.

Although Baba Bulleh Shah's poetry is extremely popular throughout both halves of Punjab, much of his published work that is available is in Shahmukhi which the Eastern Punjabis cannot read or understand so well now. The names of everyday objects are different, and people do not know much about each other's religious beliefs to understand what is being said in the poetry. There is also a lack of knowledge in the history of their region and how people used to live happily together, as most find it difficult to look back past the bloody separation of 1947.

When writing my first book, I was thinking about the new younger generation of Punjabis who have been born and grown up in the West and mainly speak English. Many of them may understand Punjabi, but few are able to read or write it. I believed translation into English would help this new generation to identify and understand their heritage and culture. In fact, what I have come to realise is that it is not just this new generation that has forgotten their mother tongue but older people too, some who even grew up in the Punjab, struggle to understand basic terms from everyday life or history of the time. Religious terms are particularly difficult to understand as people do not seem to know much about religions other than their own. This makes it difficult for some to understand comparisons being made in the poetry about other Faiths and commonality between Faiths.

As a result, many people have come back to me asking to explain the meaning behind the poems I covered. This is something I am happy to do by way of this book, which should be read as a companion to my first book, as that has the poems in the original Gurmukhi, Shahmukhi and transliteration.

I am not aware of any other book that has translated and explained the meaning in this way, of some of Baba Bulleh Shah's poetry (if there is, please let me know via the Publisher). In this book, I have further improved the translation of the forty poems I covered in my first book and also explain different terms that may not be familiar any more, highlight the history being talked about and convey the spiritual aspect of the Sufi beliefs of Baba Bulleh Shah.

Each time I read or hear a verse of Baba Bulleh Shah, I gain further insight into his message. I hope this will be the same for readers of this book as my interpretation of what is being said is not the only explanation. The aim is to give the reader a base from which to build their understanding.

It is important to understand that the words of the poetry are of Baba Bulleh Shah, but the interpretation is my own. I do not claim to be an academic of this subject and the descriptions are merely my own ideas and thoughts of what I think Baba Bulleh Shah was trying to convey.

I have been mindful not to over-explain the poems but to give enough explanation of difficult terms to point the reader in the direction of the subject matter. I hope that the reader can then research the various historical events or personalities of the time for themselves.

I believe that Baba Bulleh Shah's message deserves to be heard and understood, as it is as relevant today as it was 300 years ago. I hope the reader derives as much inspiration from the poems as I have.

Artistic impression of Baba Bulleh Shah

# 1. If God could be found (Jay Rub Mildha).

If God could be found by bathing and washing,

Then, He would have been found by frogs and fish!


If God could be found in jungles and plains,

Then, He would have been found by cows and buffalos!


If God could be found within temples and mosques,

Then, He would have been found by the old and emaciated!


O' Bullehya, God is only found,

By those who have true intentions!

In this poem, Baba Bulleh Shah describes the futility of merely performing rituals to find God, if true intention is not also present. He uses examples of rituals from Islam, Hinduism and Buddhism to convey his point.

In the first line, he mentions "bathing" and "washing". By "bathing" he is referring to the Hindu practice of bathing in the river Ganges to purify and wash away sins. In Hinduism, rivers are regarded as holy, but the Ganges is seen as the holiest of all, as it is believed to be an incarnation of the goddess Ganga, who is worshipped as the goddess of purification and forgiveness.

By "washing", Baba Bulleh Shah is referring to the ritual ablutions (wuzu), that Muslims perform before each of the five daily prayers or undertaking any religious service. Private areas, followed by hands and forearms up to elbows, face, nose, mouth, ears, top of head to back of neck and feet up to ankles are all ritually washed with water three times while reciting prayers. These ritual ablutions are essential to purify and cleanse the person before performing his religious duties. Without them, or if they are not performed correctly, the person remains un-cleansed, and his devotions may not be valid.

In the second couplet, Baba Bulleh Shah is talking about the practice of people taking to wandering in jungles, seeking solitude in uninhabited places or living as hermits far away from others, to find God. Although this practice was common to all the main religions at the time, he is including it here as part of the Buddhist tradition where adherents would try to emulate the Buddha by wandering the jungles and isolating themselves in their quest for enlightenment.

In the third couplet, Baba Bulleh Shah is highlighting the mainly elderly men who tended to congregate in temples and mosques. No longer able to do physical work in the fields, and in search of solace from women and grandchildren at home, they tended to gather in these places with other men of similar age, for company and to make it easier to go from one prayer to another. They were typically frail and emaciated-looking, with their leather-like skin stretched tight over their bones (Chum churrhickian). If God could be found by just being in mosques and temples, then these elderly men would have found Him as they spend most of their time there. It is not the amount of time spent in these places, however, which helps to find God, but having the true intention to find Him that is required.

Baba Bulleh Shah points out other creatures who do these same things naturally all the time. The same actions there are about survival, and nothing to do with finding God. The difference is intent. If rituals are performed without intent, then they are no different to these natural behaviours. Without intention, rituals are mere rituals and are worthless in finding God.

## 2. Essence (Muqeed).

If I search for You within me,

Then I know You are my essence,

If I look for You externally,

Then who pervades within me?


You are everything, You are within everyone,

I recognise You as the Holiest,

I am also You, You are also me,

Then who is this wretched Bullah?

In this poem, Baba Bulleh Shah is trying to make sense of his own nature. Like all Sufis, he believed that God is everywhere, in everything and in everyone and in fact everything in the entire Universe is part of God. Sufis use the metaphor of God as being an Ocean of Universal Love, within which everything is "floating".

Judeo-Christian-Islamic Faiths and many other world religions teach that "God created Man in His own image". This does not mean that Man looks like God, and paintings of God as an old man creating Adam, as by Michelangelo in the Sistine Chapel in the Vatican, are entirely fanciful. What the scriptures are saying is that God created Man in His own image in terms of his nature, and that the nature of God and Man are similar. As God is also literally in everything and everyone, Baba Bulleh Shah is saying that when he looks within himself, he recognises that God is there as his real essence. If this is the case, then it makes sense that we grasp this first, before searching for Him in other places. Once we have recognised Him within ourselves, then we will be able to see Him in everyone else too.

In the second Kafi, Baba Bulleh Shah reiterates his core values that God is in everything and everyone and that he sees God as the Purest and Holiest. He ends by saying that if God is in Bulleh Shah as part of his essence, then Bulleh Shah's spirit is also with God as part of His Being. If this is the case, and everything and everyone is part of God, then this perishable body of Bulleh Shah is of no significance.

## 3. Ocean of Love (Ishq Sammundur).

Living surreptitiously, then what is to be dead?

What can you become like this, and what can you accomplish?

When we have to jump into the Ocean of Love,

Then what is drowning, and what is to swim?

The word "look" in Punjabi means "to hide" and is often used in conjunction with itself to make the phrase "look, look", meaning constantly hiding, looking over one's shoulder or living secretly or surreptitiously. It is an opposite state to living your life openly and honestly and describes someone who has something to hide or has a secret that they may be worried about coming out, like their Faith, caste, politics, family background or a whole host of other things. Living like this means living a lie and constantly fearing that you will be found out and being ever ready to flee if you are exposed. Baba Bulleh Shah lived at a time of great upheaval and turbulence in the Punjab, as discussed in the chapter on his life and times in my previous book. There was famine and invasions, and a stricter, fundamental version of Islam was being implemented. These unsettled times made people fearful and afraid to speak out against injustices. Many attempts were made to silence Baba Bulleh Shah, including threats of violence, and issuing of "Fatwas" or religious edicts declaring him a heretic, but he was not cowed by these. Here, he also encourages others not to be afraid or hide from their oppressors.

In this "Kafi" (quatrain), Baba Bulleh Shah says that if you live like this, in fear, not speaking up for your rights, beliefs, truth and justice, then how is that any different to you not existing at all or being dead. To live surreptitiously like this, being fearful and constantly looking over your shoulder means that you will never be able to achieve your true potential as a human being or achieve anything worthwhile.

The "Ocean of Love" is a term used in Sufism to describe God, and within this ocean, everything that exists, ever existed or ever will exist, including Time is suspended. By "jump into the Ocean of Love" Baba Bulleh Shah is talking about the moment of death, when there will be no choice, but the tiny speck of our soul will have to jump into the vast Ocean of Universal Love. This will be far more frightening than anything that we might have to confront in life, but it will have to be done anyway. Once part of that Ocean of Love, however, nothing else will matter as we will be with God. In other words, death is the ultimate terror, but every soul will still have to experience it. If we can face death in the end, then we can face anything in life and we should not be afraid of anything or hide away from anyone.

## 4. Fragile heart (Naazuk dil).

We are people of a fragile heart,

Don't keep hurting our heart, my friend,

Don't keep making false promises,

Don't keep taking false vows!


How many times have I said to you?

Don't keep testing me moment by moment,

I will die, longing for you,

Don't make me remember you so much!

As a Sufi, Baba Bulleh Shah's greatest desire was to be able to see God and for God to reside within him. Sufis use metaphors of "Beloved" (True Love) or "Yaar" (Best Friend) to describe God as He is the ultimate True Love or Best Friend. Here Baba Bulleh Shah is complaining to his "Yaar" as to why He keeps eluding him. He says to Him that You know I am weak and my heart is fragile and easily broken, so please don't keep breaking it. Every day, Baba Bulleh Shah hopes that he will see his Beloved today, or he feels his Best Friend is bound to meet him today, but it does not happen and he is left broken-hearted. So, he implores his Best Friend to stop making these promises and vows, raising his hopes and then letting him down, breaking his heart over and over.

Baba Bulleh Shah feels he is being tested by God again and again, and does not know what else he can do to see Him. He tells Him that he is too weak to withstand these tests and to stop testing him so much.

In the final two lines, Baba Bulleh Shah says that I long for you so much that I know when I die, I will be remembering You. So, by making me remember You more and more, You are hastening my demise. In other words, You are killing me by making me long for You so much.

## 5. Rising Suns (Churrhdhay suraj).

Rising suns, we have seen setting,

Doused lamps, we have seen ignited.

No-one values a diamond,

But fake coins traded, we have seen!


Those who have no one in this world,

Even those sons, we have seen prosper.

With His grace, o man,

People walking on water, we have seen!


People moan, lentils are not softening,

Melting stones, we have seen!

Those who failed to value the Beloved, Bullehya,

Rubbing their empty hands, we have seen!

Rising suns setting and doused lamps igniting is a beautiful way of describing the passing of days and time. Each day the sun rises and each night it sets and as it sets, those lamps (Diway) in the heavens, the stars, which had been doused by it are re-ignited. This way Baba Bulleh Shah is saying that he has seen the passage of time and with this ageing is able to share what he has learnt.

Apart from the passing of time, the same analogy can be used for people. When someone is rising up in public life, it is said that his star is rising, and people congregate around him, as people worship a rising sun. Inevitably, they may fall out of favour and their star begins to fade and extinguish.

Baba Bulleh Shah was not only a Sufi mystic but also cared deeply about people and believed in social justice. In this poem he is talking about the state of society and telling people that salvation lies in holding onto and valuing God. He believed that there was widespread corruption and nepotism in the ruling classes and in offices of State and the religious orthodoxy pandered to this rich and powerful elite. It is these people he complains about in lines 3 and 4 saying that they are not capable of valuing a diamond or a worthy, able person, when appointing officials but instead promote corrupt, incompetent sycophants, by receiving bribes. Such men, Bulleh Shah compares to fake coins that are passed for the genuine article.

In the second verse, Baba Bulleh Shah reminds people that it is possible, even for those who have nothing or no-one, to prosper and thrive in this world and achieve greatness. To do this, he uses the example of Jesus, who the Bible and the Quran say, was born of Virgin birth and had no father in this world. He was blessed with many powers by God, with whose grace he performed numerous miracles including walking on water.

In Punjabi, the saying "daal nehin guldhi", literally meaning the lentils are not tenderising or softening, has another use in day-to-day life. It is also used for when people don't get their own way. This can apply to many aspects of life but typically may be when some petty bureaucrat hinders your just request in order to try and extract a bigger bribe. Baba Bulleh Shah says that these petty bureaucrats, like grains of lentils, are nothing to be feared because he has seen big rocks, i.e. more powerful governors and rulers, melt away into nothing.

In the final two lines, Baba Bulleh Shah says that he has seen those who do not value God and His commands, at their end, rubbing their empty hands in despair.

## 6. Sectarianism (Firka-bundhi).

On one side live Wahabis, the other Deobandis,

Front and back are Shia and Sunni, strong is sectarianism.

Midst of all this is our house, grim is our fate,

One neighbourhood, eight mosques, which one should we follow!

Baba Bulleh Shah lived at a time of great strife with famine and communal violence in the Punjab between Hindus, Muslims and Sikhs based on their religious differences. This caused great distress to Baba Bulleh Shah who believed in peoples living together in harmony and tolerance irrespective of their Faith, caste, race, colour or gender. He saw God in everything and everyone, regardless of any obvious differences.

Islam was also going through great upheaval at this time with rising sectarianism within its own ranks. Muslims were already divided into two major sects with the vast majority being Sunni but also a smaller but significant group, the Shia, or Party of Ali. The differences between these two were mainly political, based around who was the rightful Heir to lead the Muslims after the death of the holy Prophet Muhammed (peace be upon him).

Around the lifetime of Baba Bulleh Shah, there was an awakening within Sunnis with realisation of threats from ignorance and European Colonialism, which resulted in the birth of two different movements with the aim of taking Muslims back to the basic tenets of Islam. One of these groups was the Wahhabis, or followers of Abd al- Wahab (1703-1792) and founded in Arabia, while the other was home-grown in Deoband, Hindustan and hence labelled Deo-bundhi. Significantly, both of these new sects preached a return to a purer, more fundamental form of Islam and viewed Sufi ideas of tolerance and equality of all Faiths as suspicious and almost heretical. Brotherhood and equal standing of all Faiths as taught by various Sufi Saints from the Punjab was difficult to reconcile with this dogmatic form of Islam, which is regarded by Muslims as the only true religion. Sufism and Sufi ideas were, therefore, seen as a perversion of the true religion and attempts were made to curtail their influence by implementing Islamic Sharia (Religious) Law.

In this Kafi, Baba Bulleh Shah highlights the sectarianism between these four groups which often turned violent. People from the different sects lived separate lives, living and marrying in their own groups, having their own schools and mosques, often calling people of other sects "Kafirs" (non-believers). Feelings ran particularly high during sensitive religious occasions and could lead to violent clashes and even deaths.

These divisions, often within the same family, were painful for Baba Bulleh Shah who here is drawing attention to the sad fact that all four of these sects believe in the same One God, Prophet and Holy Book, yet they each have their own mosques where only people of their own sect may pray. Almost in despair, he says to them, tell me which mosque I should go and attend?

# 7. In a single point (Ik nuktay wich).

Grasp the point, let go of the Reckoning,

Cast aside Hell, and tortures of the grave,

Close shut the gateways of unbelief,

Cleanse pure the desires of your heart!

> In such a house the Word finds refuge,
>
> In a single point, the matter ends!

Mere prostration, is just rubbing of the ground,

Thus, gaining a marked forehead, is for showing off,

Professing the Kalma to please others,

Is not of bringing understanding in your heart!

> Can the true word ever be hidden?
>
> In a single point, the matter ends!

One goes to the jungle, another the seas,

Only eating a single grain each day,

Without understanding, weakening their bodies,

Then return home having become sickly!

> In pointless Retreats, only the body shrivels!
>
> In a single point, the matter ends!

Grasp an able Guide, so Godliness can begin,

Within you be ecstasy and care freeness,

Without want and in total contentment,

Within your heart be total clarity,

> Bullehya! can the true word ever stop?
>
> In a single point, the matter ends!

In Punjabi, the word "nukta" denotes a dot or full stop but can also mean "the point" as in the "point of view". In Shahmukhi Punjabi, which uses the Arabic script, it also refers to the dot(s) placed above or below a letter to change its sound. For example, the basic Arabic letter for B has one dot below it, but if the same letter has three dots below it, it is pronounced as a P.

The "nukta" in this poem is referring to the dot that is above the letter "Alif", the first letter of the Arabic alphabet. "Alif" is a vertical letter, pointing upwards, and looks similar to the number "one". When written fully as pronounced, it is spelt using the letters Alif, Laam and Fay. The Fay here has a dot above it, to differentiate it from B and P. Thus, the letter "Alif" is the first letter of the word "Alif" and this word "Alif" has a single dot, nukta, above it.

Apart from being the first letter of the Arabic alphabet, "Alif" is also the first letter of the word Allah, making it very powerful spiritually for Sufis. If we look at it in terms of God describing Himself as being Alpha and Omega, first and last letters of the Greek alphabet, meaning "I am the beginning and the end", then we can see how significant "Alif" is in relation to Islam as it is the first letter for Allah and denotes the "beginning" of All things. As the letter and the word "Alif" are so powerful, then the dot above it is seen, by Sufis, as the epicentre of this power, into which all matters end and there is no further debate. Looking at it another way, Allah is One, the Purest and the Holiest, the Eternal and the Ultimate, and all matters begin and end with Him. Thus, if you grasp this point then nothing else matters. If you turn to Allah, chant his name and always behave as if in His presence, then the rest will fall into place. All the differences that have been created based on religion, caste, race, colour, or gender will no longer matter.

So, we can see in this poem that the word "nukta" is being used to carry many different meanings but significantly it is being used to convey that if we grasp Allah and bring Him into our hearts, then that is all that matters.

In the first verse of this poem, Baba Bulleh Shah says exactly this; "grasp the point", in other words just grasp onto Allah and stop worrying about other things. Muslims bury their dead and believe that after burial, they will be visited by angels who will question them on their Faith. If the deceased gives them satisfactory answers, their grave will be made to feel spacious and they will feel heavenly breezes, but if they had no Faith or denied Allah, then their grave will be tightened upon them, and they will feel heat from fires of Hell. This will continue until the end of time when the Earth will be destroyed and all the dead will rise up on the Day of Judgement or the Reckoning, when each soul will have to give an account of themselves. This Reckoning or accounting determines your final abode in Paradise or in Hell for eternity.

Essentially Baba Bulleh Shah is saying that if you grasp onto and believe in One God, do not let unbelief "Kufr" into your soul and have a Pure heart, then this is all that God wants from you and you need not worry about your Reckoning, tortures of the grave or Hell. When you do this and have a pure heart, God will come and reside in it and then you will no longer transgress. When God is living in your heart, nothing more is needed, the matter is concluded.

Baba Bulleh Shah warned against following rituals thoughtlessly, without true intent to find God behind them. In this he included rituals of all different religions, and he warned against hypocrisy of all types. Conversely, it may be said that he did not have issue with rituals of any religion, if they showed belief in the Unity of One God (Tawheed), and if they were being practiced with true intention to find God. It is intent behind the rituals that separates man from animals.

In the second verse, he points out to Muslims, that without true intent, prostration (Sujda) during ritual prayers (Namaz) may as well be just rubbing of the ground! Many Muslims who perform the daily five prayers tend to develop a bruise mark on their foreheads called the "Mehrab" which some may display as a badge of honour to show others how "pious" and strict they are about prayers.

"Kalma" is the declaration of Faith that is required to be recited in front of witnesses when a person wants to join the Islamic Faith. Baba Bulleh Shah would have been aware of people converting to the Islamic Faith for their own advancement in society perhaps and says that just reciting this declaration does not bring understanding in your heart and it is mere hypocrisy to please others. Seeming to become Muslim by reciting the Kalma but carrying on as before is not something that you will be able to keep hiding.

The third verse is about people needlessly following arduous tasks in the belief that the more difficult and dangerous the venture, the more likely they are to find God. Baba Bulleh Shah talks here about people going on arduous retreats or vigils, "Chillas", which people still use to try and achieve enlightenment.

The practice of "Chillas" goes back to ancient times, the most famous of it being performed by Siddhartha Gautam, who became known as the Buddha and lived around the 6th Century BC.

Performing the "Chilla" involves the person going off on his own to the jungle, mountains or isolated islands and then spending specific lengths of time within a small, demarcated space meditating while depriving himself of food, water, sleep or other bodily functions. They may decide that they will eat one grain of lentil or a drop of water a day and spend all their time chanting or meditating. The Buddha performed his "Chilla", which typically lasted forty-nine days, under a holy tree and it took him many years to achieve Enlightenment.

Other examples of "Chillas" being performed include the Prophet Moses who after delivering the Israelites from bondage in Egypt, ascended Mount Sinai and remained there meditating for forty days before seeing God in the burning bush and receiving the Ten Commandments.

Jesus also wandered the desert for forty days and nights during which he was tempted by the Devil and rejected him.

Baba Bulleh Shah, therefore had no issue with performing of "Chillas" but once again points to performing these without direction from a Guru, or without true intent. In these cases, he says that they will never find God and will merely return home sick and emaciated with shrivelled bodies but none the wiser or closer to God.

It is not within the capabilities of everyone to devote the time and effort in solely searching for God and Sufis recognise this. The message of Baba Bulleh Shah for ordinary people is very simple; grasp Allah and have a pure heart in which He can reside so that you live a decent and fulfilled life with other human beings. For people who want to devote their lives to learn and search for God, Sufis regard the guidance of a "Murshid", a learned and able Guide or Guru as essential. This Guide can then teach you and monitor you so that you follow the correct path to finding God. Without such oversight from an able Guide, Sufis fear that you could be led astray by your own Ego (Nafs).

In the last verse, Baba Bulleh Shah entreats such a person embarking on a journey to finding God to first find a "Murshid" who can then cleanse your thoughts and begin to plant shoots of godliness. When this happens, it will bring a feeling of freedom and peace within you, and you will no longer be chasing after worldly things but be satisfied with what you have. The Guide will help you to clean your heart of damaging thoughts and make pure for God to come and dwell in it and for you to see Him.

Finally, Baba Bulleh Shah asks, can truth ever be stopped, meaning God's Will is always done and truth is always victorious.

## 8. The One sitting at home (Khur bettha).

Reading and studying, you have become a high scholar,

But you have never considered your own self,

You keep barging into temples and mosques,

But you have never entered your inner self.


For nothing are you battling with Satan every day,

When you have never fought your own ego,

Bulleh Shah! you are trying to catch those flying in the heavens,

But you have never grasped the One sitting at home!

In this poem, Baba Bulleh Shah is addressing the Muslim religious orthodoxy of his day in the form of Scholars whose duty it was to lead Muslims to the correct path and guide Rulers if they stray from Islamic Law or teaching. The first line makes it clear that he is talking to the "Alim" or Islamic Scholar(s), and particularly the high or accomplished scholars who study many years at designated religious colleges and universities. These "Alim" or plural "Ulema" are considered the guardians of religious law and morality in Sunni Muslim societies.

The word "purrh" in Punjabi literally means "to read" and when used as the phrase "purrh, purrh" implies a great deal of reading or studying. The first line of this poem is laying out that after a great amount and time of arduous learning, the "Alim" has established himself as an accomplished Scholar. Then Baba Bulleh Shah says, but you have never studied or looked at your own self. This still applies today where someone blindly rote learns extensive knowledge but lacks insight or life experience.

The life of an "Alim" revolves around the mosques and madrassas (religious schools) and similar applies to Hindu Scholars who will be found at temples and shrines. Baba Bulleh Shah says that you keep going into these places but you have not taken the trouble to look within your own inner self.

The Scholars will daily be looking for improper practices of religion or performance of incorrect rituals and declaring them as unbelief (Kufr) and stamping them out. They would regard this as doing God's work and fighting Satan (Shaitan). For example, some scholars believed then and still do now that music and dancing are un-Islamic and should be banned. For Sufis, like Baba Bulleh Shah, music and dancing was an essential part of their devotion to God and a way of reaching up to God. So, Baba Bulleh Shah is saying that you are wasting your time on issues like this, when you have not managed to control your own inner ego (Nafs), which is the true deceiver that takes us away from God.

Finally, and this is the crux of the matter, Baba Bulleh Shah says to the scholars that you are trying to catch those flying in the heavens, unreachable angels, demons, Satan, but you have never tried to grab the One sitting at home or inside you. Religious scriptures of many faiths indicate that Man is God's highest creation and the intricacies of the human body reveal God's hand at work. God also breathed life into Man and resides within him, though He may be veiled. Thus, if one only looks within himself, one can see God's design, without the need for searching for elusive flying beings like angels.

## 9. Bullehya! What I know (Bullehya! Ki Janrrhan).

Not am I a Believer, nor in mosques,

Not am I in the rituals of the Unbelievers,

Not am I in the pure, nor in the un-cleansed,

Not am I Moses, nor am I Pharaoh!

>                    Bullehya! what I know, who I am.

Not am I in notions of unclean or purity,

Not am I in happiness, nor in sorrow,

Not am I of water, nor am I of dust,

Not am I fire, nor within air!

>                    Bullehya! what I know, who I am.

Not am I in the books of Veda,

Not am I in opium, nor in alcohol,

Not in the antics of the intoxicated and corrupt,

Not in keeping awake, nor in sleeping!

>                    Bullehya! what I know, who I am.

Not I who founded the mysteries of religions,

Not am I who bore Adam and Eve,

Not I who had Myself named,

Not am I in staying put, nor in wandering,

>                    Bullehya! what I know, who I am.

I know Myself to be the First and Last,

There is no one else I acknowledge,

There is no one more capable than Me,

Bullehya! who then is left standing?

>                    Bullehya! what I know, who I am.

Baba Bulleh Shah spent his life trying to make sense of the Nature of God and how to see Him. He believed that the "Nature of God and Man is one" and he saw God being present everywhere, in everything and everyone. The reason Sufis believe we cannot see God, is because He is veiled from us by our Ego (Nafs) and this has to be defeated in order to unveil Him. The strength of the ego and how it is nourished by an individual determines the thickness of the veiling, so that if the ego is unchallenged in someone, the veil between him and God would be very thick and it would be difficult to see the presence of God in that person, even though God is still there. Sufism teaches that this ego must be overcome and destroyed if one truly wants to see God, but to achieve this, first a capable teacher (Murshid) must be found who guides you and monitors you for signs of your ego surfacing or deceiving you. Baba Bulleh Shah says of his own Murshid, Shah Innayat, that he opened his eyes to seeing God in everyone.

Every religion has conundrums within it where someone might say "but why did this happen or God allow that to happen" and there is no specific answer. Baba Bulleh Shah also grappled with these questions and tried to make sense of things in terms of religious teachings such as: God is everywhere at once, He can see and hear everything, He is in everything, He is in every one of us. Baba Bulleh Shah explained these as mysteries "Rumzanh" that only God understands and said that we should not concern ourselves with what or why He does something, but that He does as He chooses.

Baba Bulleh Shah sets this poem in the form of a riddle to himself to explain what he thinks is the Nature of God. He does not tell us what he thinks is the Nature of God, but at the end leaves it to us to work out what that Nature might be.

Even the title of this poem is ambiguous as to whether it should have an exclamation or question mark at the end of it. Most people tend to make it a question, turning it into "Bullehya! What do I know who I am?", but when the poem is read in its entirety, this being a question does not make sense. When the entire poem is read, it is clear that this is a voice of someone other than Baba Bulleh Shah, coming from within him, telling him who He is. If we take this further and say that this is his inner voice telling him the Nature of God, then that voice would not be uncertain as to who He is but is clearly telling Bulleh Shah what He is and is not. Whether the title is a question or an answer should not detract from the profound beauty and mysticism of this poem.

In the first line of the poem, the voice spells out that He is not just to be found in the Muslim Believers, "Momin", and nor is He confined to just inside mosques. He then says that neither is He in the rituals of unbelief (Kufr). He is not only in those who have ritually cleansed themselves or solely in those who have not. The voice then says that He is neither Moses nor the Pharaoh. The story of Prophet Moses and the Egyptian Pharaoh, is portrayed in Abrahamic Faiths as a battle between good and evil, with Moses and the Israelites being saved by the intervention of God. Sufis regard this as one of those Mysteries of God where God was present in both men, as He is in everyone, and in effect fought Himself in the guise of these two men. Hence the voice here saying that He is not only in Moses or only in Pharaoh.

The second verse deals with different religious ideas as to what the Nature of God might be. "Paleet" means impure and unclean, whereas "Paak" signifies purity and ritually cleansed. These notions are used in various religions, so for example in Islam, one is un-cleansed without performing ritual ablutions (Wuzu). Pigs, dogs and a whole host of other things are "unclean" that make you unclean if you touch them and require cleansing by ritual ablutions. The Caste system in Hinduism segregates people into different categories at birth, with the Brahmins being the highest caste and untouchables (Dalit) being the lowest. Non-Hindus are also categorised as Untouchables. The mere shadow of an untouchable person would make any of the higher castes unclean until they have ritually cleansed themselves. A person is born into his caste and can never shed it, bequeathing the same to all his future generations. The inner voice here is telling Baba Bulleh Shah, that He is not a part of these notions of caste, unclean and pureness.

Hindus worship the Ganges as an incarnation of the goddess Ganga and believe that bathing in the river washes away their sins and cleanses them. Others in deserts might see dust swirls as supernatural. Hindus and Zoroastrians worship fire and others see the Divine in lightening and rain. The voice says, He is not restricted to these.

In the third verse, the voice tells Baba Bulleh Shah that He did not start or found the mystery of religions, nor did He give birth to Adam and Eve. The voice denies even having itself named. This is a reference to the fact that in Judaism, which is the root of both Christianity and Islam, the Israelites were never instructed to call God by any particular name but instead were guided by Moses to address

Him with the title "Yahweh", meaning "I Am that I Am" or "I Am the One Who Is". In the Middle Ages, Christian monks changed this title to "Jehovah". In Islam "Allah" is a title and not a name for God meaning "The One God". Interestingly, Muslims have 99 names for God, which are really His attributes such as "All-Merciful", "All-Forgiving".

So, the inner voice is telling Baba Bulleh Shah that He did not start religions or their rules and rituals and that He did not even give Himself a name to be known by. Then, once again, the voice says it is not to be found only in actions of sitting like a hermit, performing "Chillas" in one spot, or wandering in jungles and plains or other isolated unreachable places.

Having laid out what He is not, the voice then tells Baba Bulleh Shah, what His nature is. The voice tells Bulleh Shah that He knows Himself to be the First and Last, i.e., the beginning and the end or all eternity. He is One and does not acknowledge anyone else equal to Him (Tawheed). He is the One that runs the Universe and everything within it and there is no one more capable than Him of doing this. The voice then asks Bulleh Shah and through him the readers and listeners to say what then is left to describe Him.

## 10. Dogs are higher than you (Kuttay tehthoon uttay)!

You awake nights, and declare yourself a Scholar,

Awake every night are dogs: they are higher than you!


From barking, their mouths never shut,

Though they be beaten: they are higher than you!


The doorway of their master they never desert,

Though they sleep on rubbish heaps: they are higher than you!


Bulleh Shah! Go and you acquire some good deeds too,

Otherwise, the dogs have won the game: they are higher than you!

A "Shaikh" in Islam is a learned religious Scholar who has studied religious law and Divinity at designated seminaries over many years. Being a "Shaikh-ul-Islam" is a highly honourific position in Muslim society and gives the bearer of the position significant powers to pronounce on matters of Faith. A religious edict, "Fatwa", is the ultimate sanction that he can apply whereby he has the power to declare someone as having left the Islamic Faith and become an unbeliever (Kafir); akin to excommunication in Roman Catholicism. Having such a religious edict issued against oneself was not only a disaster for the person who thus became "persona non grata" but brought shame on the entire family.

Having such power to be able to discharge someone from the Faith, could also be misused in the wrong hands. Power such as this can corrupt people and it was the view of many, including Baba Bulleh Shah, that many of these Scholars, Shaikhs and Alims, were corrupt and easily bribed by the rich and powerful to do their bidding. They were also used by Rulers and Governors to control dissent or criticism of them, in return for financial reward.

Sufi Saints such as Hazrat Sultan Bahoo (1629-1691) had already recognised and spoken out against the corruption of the religious orthodoxy, but Baba Bulleh Shah took this message further. The great Sufi Saints were always a barometer of the feeling of the ordinary peoples' views, and people generally mistrusted the ruling elites or religious leaders and felt they were all corrupt. They felt there was no justice for the common person and that the rich and powerful did as they pleased. If someone tried to voice these concerns, they were treated extremely harshly with all the powers of state including issuing of religious edicts to keep them in line.

One of the reasons the Sufi Saints were and are so influential is because they saw the plight of the people and put voice to their concerns through their poetry. By understanding and highlighting the plight of the poor people, Sufi Saints in effect became their voice and gathered huge followings which in turn protected the Saints to some extent from retribution by the State authorities and religious orthodoxy. Still, it was a difficult role, and many Sufis paid for it with their lives. Baba Bulleh Shah was himself censured many times and had many "Fatwas" issued against him, including some declaring him an unbeliever. At a time when Rulers could be as bloodthirsty as they liked, to become a Sufi Saint was not a choice for the weak-hearted and Baba Bulleh Shah never let himself be cowered by any threats and always spoke out against injustice of any kind.

Apart from religious censure by the orthodoxy, Baba Bulleh Shah faced constant threat of violence. He was physically beaten on occasion and is known to have had to take refuge in a Gurdwara to escape his attackers. This Gurdwara Sahib at Daftu in Kasur,

Pakistan is still present but in a great state of disrepair, having partially collapsed following heavy monsoon rains in 2023.

This is one of Baba Bulleh Shah's most famous poems and maybe his response to the religious orthodoxy that hounded him. It is still loved by people and recited with great feeling today.

In Muslim society, dogs are unclean animals, and their roles are reserved for guarding or hunting. Touching a dog makes one "unclean" requiring the person to ritually purify before undertaking any other roles. Calling someone a dog is to call them the lowest of the low. In this poem, Baba Bulleh Shah compares the religious Shaikhs to the lowly dog and says that even these dogs are better than you. He compares the natural behaviours and instincts of dogs to those of the Shaikhs and says that dogs come out on top.

Firstly, he says that just because you stay up at night to study or contemplate, you have yourself declared a great Shaikh, but look at the dogs who are awake all night but are not honoured in any way. So just comparing waking at night is of no consequence because the dogs are doing it without motive, compared to you doing it for a purpose which is to be called a Scholar.

The dogs do not stop from barking and doing their duty even if they are rewarded with sleeping on a rubbish tip. This means that dogs will continue to do their duty to bark, even if there is no reward and they must sleep on a rubbish tip, unlike the Shaikhs who in order to get comfort and monetary gain, will stop speaking up against injustice and do as they are told by the rich and powerful. Again, Baba Bulleh Shah says, dogs are higher in morals then them.

Dogs are very loyal animals and will stick with their master through thick and thin. They never abandon their master no matter how much they might be mistreated or beaten. Baba Bulleh Shah compares this to the Shaikhs who to save their own skin will turn and betray God if the rich and powerful ask or pay them to do this.

In the end, Baba Bulleh Shah tells these Shaikhs to take some sense and start doing some good also, otherwise, he warns them that the dogs have won the game.

## 11. Inside and out (Undher, baahr).

Don't lose your temper,

Let things cool before eating,

Your days too, will swing around,

Don't fret for no reason!

Sow plants of such love,

That you provide shade for the whole village,

Destroy falsehood from within yourself,

Always beat the drum of truth!

Having eaten scraps of food,

Prostrate yourself in humble gratitude,

Sweep your inner self with a broom,

Cleanse your inside and out!

Baba Bulleh Shah lived through very difficult times in the history of Punjab with war, hunger, famine, drought and sectarian violence. In this poem, he gives a message of hope to the ordinary people who may have felt they had been abandoned to a life of misery.

The message Baba Bulleh Shah gives them is very pragmatic in that times will change for the better and to not lose hope.

He tells people not to lose their tempers, or be incited, as anger clouds judgement and leads to further discord. "Let things cool before eating" means to think about things before acting rather than lashing out without considering the facts. He tells them that these bad times will not last forever and that things will turn around and get better so not to lose hope and fret needlessly.

The way to do this, Baba Bulleh Shah tells them is to stick together and support each other. To do good things and good deeds which will grow like plants and provide shade and shelter for the whole village. He tells them to destroy lies and hatred from within themselves and always act truthfully and without malice towards others.

Food may be scarce, but Baba Bulleh Shah says to be thankful for whatever you get, and bow down to God with gratitude. Just like sweeping your house, get a broom of faith and hope and sweep your inner self too, getting rid of hatred and malice.

## 12. Neither am I Hindu (Hindu nanh-hinh, nanh Mussalmaan).

Neither am I Hindu, nor a Muslim,

Lose all your pride in the flowing rivers.


Neither are we Sunni, nor are we Shia,

Love for all, is the path we have adopted.


Neither hungry, nor are we sated,

Neither naked, nor are we covered.


Neither weeping, nor are we laughing,

Neither abandoned, nor are we wedded.


Neither sinners, nor are we unblemished,

Path of sinful belief, we do not follow.


Bulleh Shah! When loss and defeat is inflicted,

Hindu and Muslim, both suffer alike!

Religious differences were not of importance to Baba Bulleh Shah who preached a message of humanity and living together in harmony regardless of your Faith, caste, race, colour, gender or background. He saw God in everything and in everyone and explained the differences in terms of God's Mysteries in trying to remain hidden from us. The rituals and practices of religions were secondary to his philosophy and this upset many in the Muslim orthodoxy who tried to declare him an unbeliever (Kafir).

The religious orthodoxy and their followers would have been spreading many rumours about Baba Bulleh Shah, as to what is his background, caste, sect and beliefs. They would have portrayed him as a heretic who put all religions on equal par. Was he Muslim, Hindu, Sikh or something else entirely?

In this poem, Baba Bulleh Shah answers these critics and fearlessly declares that he is neither Hindu, nor Muslim but is a true lover of God. He says that calling yourself one or the other is a matter of pride and he does not want to be a part of that division.

In the second couplet he says that he is neither Sunni nor Shia. To Baba Bulleh Shah, these two sects of Islam were a source of disharmony and division between people and he did not want to be part of either of them. Instead, he declares that he has taken the path of love for all whatever their beliefs.

Baba Bulleh Shah then describes his own way of living where neither does he fast or starve but neither does he over-indulge or eat in excess. For clothing he only needs basic to cover his needs of modesty and weather. Here he advocates a modest lifestyle, rejecting greed and materialism, still so prevalent today.

In the fourth couplet he describes his state of mind that he is neither gloomy and despondent nor is he jovial and celebrating the current state in his land. He says that he is not wedded to a family, but he is not alone or left abandoned either as his Shrine constantly welcomes people of all backgrounds who may come and partake of free food (Lungar) there.

Baba Bulleh Shah denies being a sinner but admits that he is not unblemished, like all fellow human beings. He says he does know or follow any belief that causes him to commit sin against God.

Finally, Baba Bulleh Shah declares that when any catastrophe occurs, does it not affect Hindus and Muslims alike? Tragedy and disaster do not separate on the basis of someone's religion but affects all in its path.

## 13. By going to Mecca (Mukkay gaiyan).

By going to Mecca, the matter is not ended,

Even if we return having prayed hundreds of Friday prayers!


By going to the Ganges, the matter is not ended,

Even if we submerge ourselves hundreds of times!


By going to Gyan, the matter is not ended,

Even if we have hundreds of prayers chanted there!


Bulleh Shah! the matter can only be ended,

When we lose the "Me" from our hearts!

Mecca, in modern day Saudi Arabia, is the holiest site in Islam and is where Muslims believe Prophet Abraham built the first House of God, the Kaaba. It is also the city where Prophet Mohammed (peace be upon him) was born. A pilgrimage to Mecca (the Hajj) is an obligation on all adult Muslims if they have the means and are able physically, to perform at least once in their lifetime and is one of the five Pillars of Islam. Although Mecca can be visited anytime (Umrah), the Hajj only occurs during specific dates of a specific month, once a year. For Muslims, it is a way of visiting the House of God and atoning for their sins and asking God for forgiveness. Many Muslims see the performing of the Hajj as a pinnacle of their devotion to God and believe that if they are there in Mecca and beg God, then all their sins will be forgiven. The Hajj lasts ten days, of which the last Friday is particularly significant as this is a holy day for Muslims during which the weekly Friday Sermon is proclaimed to Muslims.

In this poem, Baba Bulleh Shah is pointing out that merely performing a particular ritual, whether you are a Muslim, Hindu or Buddhist does not guarantee anything unless you have true intentions and repent from your heart.

In the first line, he tells Muslims that just going to Mecca to merely perform various rituals does not end the matter (Gul) or achieve ultimate salvation, unless you go with true intent and repent. Merely visiting Mecca is not sufficient even if we stay there to complete hundreds of Friday prayers.

The river Ganges is holy for Hindus as it is believed to be an incarnation of the goddess Ganga. Hindus believe that submerging oneself in the river cleanses and washes away their sins. Baba Bulleh Shah says that do not think these acts of submersion will do anything unless you truly repent, no matter if you submerged yourself hundreds of times.

Gyan is a mythical holy kingdom located in the Himalayas and has been referred to in many Buddhists texts as a place of pilgrimage. Its actual location is unknown and only accomplished saints devoid of sins may be able to locate it. Baba Bulleh Shah says that even if you find and reach this place of veneration and have hundreds of prayers offered there, it is still not a guarantee of salvation.

Finally, baba Bulleh Shah tells us, what would be required to end the matter and deliver us from our sins and that is true repentance and destruction of our own ego. It is this ego which keeps us veiled from God and unless controlled and annihilated, will continue to misguide us, no matter how many pious rituals we perform.

## 14. It is just You (Tuhiyoon ain)!

It is just You, there's no me, my friend,

It is just You, there's no me!


Image of an empty ruin, my mind is no longer spinning,

If I speak, You speak with me, if I stay silent, my mind does not!

If I sleep, You sleep with me, if I walk You are the way,

Bullehya! My Love has come into my house, my life I give as offering to Him!


It is just You, there's no me, my friend,

It is just You, there's no me!

Sufis ultimately desire to be one with God so that He shines through their every word and action. They are aware that God is present in everything and in everyone but He cannot be seen. It is very arduous to lift the veil created by our ego and true Sufis must suffer many trials and tribulations to annihilate it. Only then through the help of an able Guru (Murshid)! Without the mentorship of such a learned teacher, the ego can easily divert the seeker from the true path. Baba Bulleh Shah recognised this and had complete faith in his Murshid, Shah Innayat, to keep him on the straight path. He says, in another poem, that he knew God was present in everyone but his Murshid gave him the eyes to be able to see it!

In this poem, Baba Bulleh Shah tells us of the emotion he feels when he can "see" God in himself and in everyone and everything. This is a profound realisation that there is nothing else but God and that everything is part of Him. This realisation makes Baba Bulleh Shah understand that our perishable, destructible bodies are not of any significance and all of nature, time and space are connected and all are part of God. Nothing is separate or independent of God and He runs everything.

In the main Kafi, Baba Bulleh Shah uses the word "Kholla", Punjabi for an empty, derelict, roofless ruin, to describe his own body without God. Everything he does and thinks and perceives is done by his spirit and this spirit is part of God and this is what matters. This is the lesson that the lifting of the veil teaches him.

When Baba Bulleh Shah has been able to shed the veil, his thoughts become more intense and clearer and are no longer clouded by intrusive, self-serving ideas just like a derelict ruin which has been stripped to its bare walls, roofless and without inhabitants. In this state of oneness with God, excluding all other thoughts, Baba Bulleh Shah recognises the pure thoughts that come from God and emanate through him when speaking but they do not stop even when he is silent as his mind continues to dwell on God. When asleep, his thoughts sleep also and wherever he walks, God is guiding him.

This is the state Baba Bulleh Shah had been searching for and now that he has achieved it, the veil has been lifted and the Beloved has finally come into his heart. This is what he had wanted and now that it has happened, he wants to offer the rest of his life to Him.

## 15. Raze the temple (Mandir dha dhai).

Raze the temple, raze the mosque,

Raze whatever can be toppled,

Only, never break a person's heart,

For God resides within hearts!

This is one of Baba Bulleh Shah's most well-known, often-quoted Kafis and is laden with his profound sense of love, harmony, tolerance and of humanity first.

As I have said in many other places in this book, Baba Bulleh Shah lived through very turbulent times in the history of the Punjab. The Mughal Empire had started a slow decline with more power resting in hands of bloodthirsty local rulers and Governors. Law and order had declined and there was threat of famine and starvation. Sectarian tensions between communities were high leading to outbreaks of communal violence. Tit for tat violence and destruction of holy places like temples and mosques, which fuelled it, was happening more and more.

Baba Bulleh Shah, saw temples and mosques as functionary buildings, built by men to facilitate their worship of God through their various Faiths. The buildings, per se, were not of importance to him, but the worship that was carried out was of real importance. He did not believe that a single human life should be lost on the basis of damage caused to a building, whether mosque or temple, and that human life was worth more than any building. He knew that buildings can be re-built, but a person cannot be brought back once killed.

In this poem, Baba Bulleh Shah addresses people who advocate destruction of a place of worship like a temple or mosque, in order to achieve discord and violence between communities. He defiantly tells them to go ahead and destroy these temples and mosques and any other man-made structure if they please, because these structures in themselves do not matter. They are just buildings; it is people that are important and should not be harmed.

Crucially he tells them though, that never break a person's heart, because this is where God truly lives. In other words, never hurt or harm a person, or break his heart because this is where our Faith truly lies, whatever Faith that might be. The true damage done when destroying places of each other's worship is not in the destruction of the building but the pain and hurt it causes in the person of that Faith, that his beliefs which he holds so dear, have not been valued.

Having respect for differences and accepting them is a crucial part of Sufism which advocates worship of One True God, in any way one chooses, without fear or suppression. By teaching people not to break someone's heart, Baba Bulleh Shah is teaching them to respect other people's beliefs and not to suppress or parody them.

## 16. Enough of your learning o' friend (Ilmoon bus kurrinh o' yaar)!

Enough of your learning o' friend, an "Alif" is all you require!

Religious knowledge is never-ending,

But there is no certainty when you might die,

An "Alif"' is all you require,

Enough of your learning o' friend!

                    Enough of your learning o' friend!

Reading and writing books, you form heaps,

Mounds of books surround you,

Surrounding you is moonlight, but within is darkness,

Ask for the "way" and you have no notion!

                    Enough of your learning o' friend!

You spend ritual prayers by adding extras,

Loud are your calls to prayer,

You climb the pulpit to shout out sermons,

Such knowledge has ruined you!

                    Enough of your learning o' friend!

Doctrines have created more differences,

Those with eyes are totally blinded,

They seize the innocent and spare the thief,

In both Worlds may they be losers!

                    Enough of your learning o' friend!

Reading much, you have yourself called a scholar,

You make up complex edicts sitting at home,

You feed off the loot from the ignorant,

You turn false oaths into true!

Enough of your learning o' friend!

Reading much, the cleric becomes a judge,

But God is pleased even without such learning,

It's your greed that pushes you day by day,

You have been ruined by your greed!

Enough of your learning o' friend!

You relish recounting religious conundrums,

You eat the food earned of creating suspicion and doubt,

You say one thing but do another,

Within you is falseness, outside is piety!

Enough of your learning o' friend!

When I learnt the lesson of True Love,

Seeing the river of Universal Unity, I entered,

I got stuck in the swirling currents of confusion,

Shah Innayat brought me across!

Enough of your learning o' friend!

An "Alif" is all you require!

The word "Ilim" in Punjabi means "to know" and can apply to all knowledge and learning. In this poem, however, it is used in the context of religious knowledge and learning, with Baba Bulleh Shah addressing the religious orthodoxy who obtain and use this knowledge for their own worldly benefits and to gain power. Baba Bulleh Shah was suspicious of these so-called religious experts as he saw their hypocrisy and corruption at first hand, but unlike the ordinary people, was not afraid to call it out. The title is almost dismissive of the knowledge of these self-styled religious experts and tells them that their drive for such learning is merely based on greed so that they can progress to higher ranks and demand larger bribes for themselves. He tells them that God does not require such learning and would be just as happy if they only grabbed onto and understood one "Alif" (A for Allah).

In the first line, Baba Bulleh Shah says that there is no limit or end to the learning of religious knowledge and it cannot be acquired by any one in its entirety. Our lives, on the other hand are very short and precarious and can end any time. Who knows if we can live out the next hour? So, it is impossible for us to learn all religious knowledge, even if we devoted our whole life to the task. This is not something that everyone can do and Baba Bulleh Shah recognises that people have to live their own lives, have families, work, live a full life, so it is not possible to do both. His answer is that if we only hold onto just A for Allah and let Allah guide our daily life and actions, then that is all that is required for us.

In the second verse, Baba Bulleh Shah describes the lifestyle of a typical religious scholar. He describes someone who reads and reads, writing tons of books, papers and theses. He is always surrounded by large volumes of books piled up all around him. But Baba Bulleh Shah says that this is to create an image of being learned and being surrounded by light whereas inside them is really darkness and ignorance. If someone was to ask them to show them "the way", they would have no clue as they have not understood what they have been learning.

The third verse is about hypocrites who use religion to appear pious to their fellows. Muslims are obligated to perform five daily ritual prayers (Namaz) which constitute certain number of prostrations (touching the forehead to the ground as submission to Allah). Within each Namaz, a fixed number of prostrations must be performed and are compulsory (Farz). On top of these, some more may be performed which are by way of example set by Prophet Muhammed (peace be upon him) and are called "Sunnat". Most Muslims would limit their ritual prayers to these farz and sunnats but, there is no limit to how many prayers may be performed in each Namaz. These further extras are called "Nuffal" and are up to the individual's preference. It can be seen that some people may choose to perform these extras to show their piety, and these are the type of people Baba Bulleh Shah is addressing here.

The calls to prayers in Islam, "Azans", are called "Baangan" in Punjabi and the "Mimbar" is the pulpit from which the Imam pronounces the Sermons.

In the third verse, therefore, Baba Bulleh Shah is addressing people who show fake religious piety by visibly and deliberately extending their ritual prayers by adding extras and who are eager to volunteer to shout out the call to prayer. By talking about climbing the "Mimbar" to shout out sermons, Baba Bulleh Shah is talking about the clerics who perform and relish these opportunities to admonish others. He says that such learning has deluded these people away from the true meaning.

In the fourth verse, Baba Bulleh Shah says that doctrines have created more differences between people because of the different ways the knowledge has been interpreted and used. In this way its interpretation has blinded some people so that they may have eyes but are blinkered by their dogma. In the third line, "they seize the innocent and spare the thief", Baba Bulleh Shah is pointing towards the corruption of the Qazis (Muslim Judges) who could easily be swayed by bribes, and he curses these people to be losers in this world and the next.

In the fifth verse, Baba Bulleh Shah talks about the self-styled scholars who by rote learning in religious schools, declare themselves religious scholars (Shaikhs, Alims). He accuses such scholars of inventing complex religious edicts without much understanding. By doing this and then using these to influence ignorant people, they earn the money to feed their avarice. Such people he says, would have no hesitation in swearing false oaths to prove true.

The sixth verse is about the greed of this religious class and Baba Bulleh Shah talks about the "Mullan", a basically-trained cleric of a village mosque, who desperately tries to study just so he can become a "Qazi", a Muslim Judge. He tells this "Mullan" that he is not doing this study of knowledge in the way of God because God is happy with people even without this study. Baba Bulleh Shah points out that he is doing this study because of his personal greed knowing that when he becomes a "Qazi", he will be able to make a lot more money from bribes. This avarice drives him daily, and has ruined him.

In the seventh verse, Baba Bulleh Shah talks about the religious orthodoxy and elite and says that they study to find complex conundrums in religion and citing these to people create an air of uncertainty in the right and wrong way of doing things. Although you teach one thing but you yourself do what suits you. Inside these people is fakeness but they show themselves as righteous.

In the last verse, Baba Bulleh Shah describes his own epiphany whereby when he learnt the lesson of True Love and entered the river of Universal Oneness, he floundered also. But then he found his Murshid, Shah Innayat, who helped him through these powerful currents and brought him across.

## 17. Someone ask (Koi puccho)!

Someone ask the Sweetheart, what does He do?

>Whatever He does, so He does!

In the mosque, He spends ritual prayers,

>then shows up in the temple!

Himself alone, yet in millions of homes,

>He is the Master of each one!

By dwelling happily in just one house,

>He cannot stay veiled!

Whomever I look at, He is there,

>He accompanies everyone!

In the river of Universal Oneness, can be seen,

>The entire world floating!

Bullehya! the love of my Master is cunning,

>it enters the blood and grazes on the flesh!

Someone ask the Sweetheart, what does He do?

>Whatever He does, so He does!

This poem addresses the mysteries of God that lead one to ask, "What does God do", "why does God do this" or "why does God let this happen"? The answer invariably is that these things are beyond our understanding and God does as He pleases. Here, Baba Bulleh Shah tries to make sense of some of these mysteries (Rumzanh) that puzzle him.

Firstly, Baba Bulleh Shah does not believe that God is present only in Believers (Momin) or in mosques alone, but He is present amongst all people of all Faiths and even no Faith at all. Hence in line three, he says that the Sweetheart (Dilbar) is present in those performing ritual prayers in mosques, but then also presents Himself in the temple (Buut-khanna or house of idols).

In line five, Baba Bulleh Shah says that although God is One, He is the one being worshipped in all these places of worship and is the Master of each one of these. Apart from places of worship, each person has God within it as a part of his essence, and hence, is also a house (Ghur) of God. Since there are billions of people, He is the Master of these billions of homes too.

The word "Purdah" in Punjabi means "Veiling" or "to be veiled" and is commonly applied to veils or clothing worn by women to cover their modesty. But "Purdah" has another concept in Hindu and Muslim societies whereby women can only appear unveiled in front of certain, close, adult male relatives, but must cover themselves in front of others.

In lines seven and eight, Baba Bulleh Shah is pointing out that just like living in one house, women cannot be in "Purdah" from their closest, so there should be no veiling between a person and God living within one body. But since God wants to remain veiled from us and not show Himself, He does not show up in a mosque or a temple or an individual, otherwise the veil would be removed and He would be visible to all. This is why, in lines nine and ten, Baba Bulleh Shah says that whomever he looks at, whatever faith, caste, colour, he sees God accompanying them.

The concept of everything being part of God and with God is described in Sufism as the river of Universal Oneness and once we understand this, Baba Bulleh Shah says we can see that the whole universe is suspended withing God. He says that this love for God is very cunning because whoever falls for it, forgets eating and drinking and wastes away physically but nourished spiritually by this love.

So, the answer to why does God do this or that is that He does as He pleases and it is all a game He plays to keep Himself hidden from us.

# 18. What repentance (Kaissi toba)?

What repentance is this repentance?  Don't repent like this my friend!


Repentance on your lips, but not from your heart,

From such repentance, you don't give up your ways,

What negligence has veiled you from seeing,

Why would the All-forgiving, give you forgiveness?

                              Don't repent like this my friend!

He donates to us a sown, sack-cloth cloak,

To get one-up on the rich and powerful,

How can he attain Muslim character?

He who has such attributes!

                              Don't repent like this my friend!

Where forbidden, there you go,

You consume by deceit, what rightfully belongs to others,

A hundred books you carry on your head,

How can you even be trusted?

                              Don't repent like this my friend!

Oppressors are not afraid of oppressing,

They die of their own doings,

Neither do they have fear of God,

Here, there, they be disgraced!


What repentance is this repentance? Don't repent like this my friend!

In Islam, the word for repentance is "Toba", and is seen as one of God's greatest gifts to humanity. True repentance is said to be loved by God so much that He may forgive all your sins and one of the titles of God is "Al-Ghuffar" or "All-Forgiving".

The first verse addresses hypocrites who constantly declare "Toba" (God forgive me), almost in every sentence, without ever changing their ways or thinking about what they are doing. It is almost as though they think that just by saying this, they will be forgiven because God is All-Forgiving. Baba Bulleh Shah tells them that they are misleading themselves if they think that they will be forgiven just for asking for forgiveness without correcting their ways. True repentance requires acknowledgement of misdeeds and true intention to never repeat them.

In the second verse, Baba Bulleh Shah talks about the true meaning of charity and being a Muslim. The word "Sufi" itself is thought to describe someone who keeps nothing for himself but shares everything with others. This was the conduct of the holy Prophet Muhammed (Peace be upon him) and of the subsequent four heirs or Caliphs of Islam. Wealth was not hoarded but shared out between people and this was to be the basis of being Muslim. Here, Baba Bulleh Shah describes people who perform charity to show-off their own generosity to other wealthy people, by giving out meagre or poor quality things to the poor. They wear rich cloths themselves and give sackcloth as charity to the poor. Baba Bulleh Shah says that these are not the characteristics of a true Muslim.

In the third verse, Baba Bulleh Shah refers to people that preach one thing but do another. Such religious scholars tell people how to live, what to do, where to go or not go. For example, they might forbid others from listening to music, dancing or drinking alcohol, but they themselves do as they please. They have no qualms conning what belongs to others by knowing legal matters from hundreds of books they carry around in their heads. These people cannot be trusted.

In the final verse, Baba Bulleh Shah talks about the corrupt and blood thirsty rulers who have no regard for life or justice. He says that these people are not afraid of oppressing others and neither are they afraid of God. They will die of their own doings, i.e., die the same violent deaths that they inflicted on others. Baba Bulleh Shah curses such people and says that may they be disgraced in this world and the next.

## 19. Accomplished Teacher (Kamil Murshid).

People keep urging Bulleh,

> you go and sit in the mosque!

Within mosques what can happen,

> if the prayer is not intended from your heart?

What can happen from external cleansing,

> if impurity remains within?

Without an accomplished Teacher, Bullehya,

> for nothing is your performed worship!

In this poem, Baba Bulleh Shah, impresses on his audience, the importance of finding and following the guidance of an able guru (Murshid). Sufis believe that without such a guide, our ego (Nafs), can mislead us and we can turn onto the wrong path. The Murshid, being independent of the disciple, can monitor and guard against the tricks his ego might play in misleading him. He also teaches his disciple how to meditate to create peace and stillness in his heart for God to make a home. Baba Bulleh Shah says of himself that although he had eyes, it was his Murshid, Shah Innayat, who gave them the ability to be able to see God accompanying everyone.

When Baba Bulleh Shah became a follower of the ideology of Universal Oneness and started teaching acceptance of differences in paths to finding God, fellow Muslims would have been concerned about his commitment to the Islamic Faith. He was born a "Sayyid", or direct descendant of the family of the holy Prophet (peace be upon him), and would have been expected to behave in a particular pious way and people would have been concerned about him going astray from his religion. Their typical advice would have been to go and set up in the mosque with other old men of his age, and concern himself with ritual prayers and reading the Quran.

Baba Bulleh Shah replies to these people by asking what can happen by being in a particular building if the prayer is not intended from the heart? It is the intent behind the prayer that matters, not the building you are in. Just being in the mosque does not ensure that your prayer will be accepted if it is just performed as a ritual.

Similarly, carrying out ritual ablutions (Wuzu) to purify external parts of the body does not cleanse the impurity from within. What is more important is to cleanse our inner selves and make them pure.

Finally, Baba Bulleh Shah says that it is to teach this difference between doing things blindly in a ritualistic way, and truly understanding the aims of worship, that an able Teacher is required. Without having that oversight and insight, a person may carry on performing rituals and prayers but they will be of no value if they are not done with the true aim behind them.

## 20. Just chant "Alif" (Ik "Alif" purrho)!

Just chant "Alif", it is a release for you!

From one "Alif" became two, three, and four,

They then became thousands of millions,

From there, they became uncountable,

The point of this "Alif" is without compare,

> Just chant "Alif", it is a release for you!

Why are you reading a mass of books?

Why does your countenance resemble executioners?

Carrying on your head, a heavy bundle of torment,

For the way ahead, is difficult and hard,

> Just chant "Alif", it is a release for you!

Without a "Hafiz", you memorize the Quran,

You keep uttering prayers to cleanse your speech,

But your focus is on your own profit,

Your mind is spinning like a circular saw,

> Just chant "Alif", it is a release for you!

Baba Bulleh Shah cared about humanity above all and wanted all his fellow Punjabis to live in peace and security and in harmony with each other. He recognised that peoples' lives were extremely hard and could be cut short anytime and wished for them to live their lives to their full potential. This included fulfilment of their commitments that living a full life involves like working, having families, education, travelling, recreation and enjoying their old age. He did not advocate people living a monastic lifestyle, in constant prayer and not participating in society. If someone wanted to adopt a life of prayer or solitude, that was for him, but obviously most people in society just want to live their normal lives. After all, if everyone in society became a monk or a hermit, then society would not survive. So, his advice to these ordinary people was to live their lives as God intended with peace, harmony and love between each other.

Baba Bulleh Shah understood that when people have such tenuous, hard lives, their priority is to work and feed their families. Farmers, as most of the Punjabis were at the time, had to work from before dawn to after sunset in order to ensure a harvest and it was only the old or disabled who could have the luxury of sitting in a mosque or temple to contemplate.

So, Baba Bulleh Shah taught people that this was fine, they were not expected to live lives of Saints in prayer but to live their lives and remember God at the same time. He urged them to just grasp onto and chant "Alif" (first letter of Allah) whenever they could. Chanting something repeatedly to focus your mind on that and let that entity into your inner self is a practice in many religions worldwide. Hindus and Buddhists chant their most sacred mantra "Om" and believe this incantation to be the sound of the Universe. Hence by chanting it repeatedly, one tries to become entuned with the sound of the Universe.

As explained in another poem, "Alif", the first letter of the Arabic alphabet is also the first letter of the word "Allah". Sufis place a great emphasis on this and believe that repeatedly chanting (Zikr) "Alif" or "Allah" brings one closer to God. Chanting is not an arduous process and can be done anytime and anywhere, even while performing other daily tasks. Baba Bulleh Shah, therefore, urges people to not worry about studying tomes of religious books or perform arduous vigils and exhaust themselves but to just focus on this one letter and grasp it's meaning.

In the first verse, Baba Bulleh Shah describes how powerful this letter "Alif" is with its unique point above the letter "fay" in Arabic, because it represents "Allah" who created and manages the whole Universe. According to Abrahamic Faiths, God created the first man, Adam, from dust and clay and breathed life into him and placed him in the Garden of Eden to live. When God wanted to create a soulmate for Adam, He did not do the same process again but created Eve from Adam himself and some of the breath that God had breathed into Adam, gave her life too.

After expulsion from the Garden of Eden, Adam and Eve had children and each time a part of the spirit from the parents was transferred into the offspring to give them life. Thus, the one breath of God that gave life to Adam, was then shared with Eve, i.e., became two, and from then on has divided exponentially to the billions of souls today. But all the spirits originate from that one breath put into Adam. So, Baba Bulleh Shah is saying look how powerful that one breath of God is, and how powerful Allah is. So, if we even chant and grasp onto the first letter of the word for Allah, that is all we need.

In the second verse, Baba Bulleh Shah, addresses the religious orthodoxy, asking them why they are making the message of Love, so complicated and frightening? Why do they study so many books looking for new and ingenious ways of suffering the sinners will endure? Why do they go on about infinite punishments of Hell or the tortures of the grave? He says that reading all these books about tortures and punishments has made them look frightening like executioners. Carrying these heavy burdens of religious knowledge is going to make it difficult for them in their progress through the next world.

Baba Bulleh Shah says in the final verse that he knows many of these scholars are charlatans. Memorizing the entire Quran (Hifz), is a great honour many Muslims aspire to. But it is not an easy task and takes a long time with teaching from a person who has already achieved this honour, (a Hafiz), to be able to do it correctly. But Baba Bulleh Shah says that these so-called scholars are self-taught and, therefore, not aware of errors they may be making. They typically make a great show of reciting prayers before performing any actions to make it look like they are cleansing their speech and will be truthful, but their real focus is on their own benefit of getting paid or fed. Even while saying these blessings, their mind is spinning elsewhere, trying to find ways of how to get more out of ignorant people.

# 21. Let it be (Bus kur ji)!

Let it be, now let it be,

Just one thing, live with us happily!


You dwell within my heart,

Why then, do you run away from us,

Yet, with powerful magic you seize our heart,

> Let it be, now let it be!

You were beating ones, who were already dead,

Cudgelling us with Kaidho's walking-stick,

You were strangling the necks of those speaking up,

Now shoot us with your well-aimed arrows!

> Let it be, now let it be!

You are trying to run, but we have grabbed you,

You are tied to us, with a lock of hair,

You are still looking for ways to hide,

Now, there is no escape by running away!

> Let it be, now let it be!

Bulleh! my Master, I am your slave,

I am dying to see your face,

I beseech You countless times,

Now come and sit deep in my chest!

> Let it be, now let it be!

In this poem, Baba Bulleh Shah is addressing his Beloved, saying enough is enough, just come and live inside me. He tells Him that He already dwells in his heart, so why does He keep running away from him, leaving him with doubts. He is frustrated with these games the Beloved keeps playing where He keeps deserting Baba Bulleh Shah, but does not leave him alone and keeps tugging at his heart drawing him to Himself.

Sufis use examples from folk tales of true lovers who died rather than give up on their love. The tragic story of Heer and Ranjha is the most famous of these from the Punjab. The two lovers were of a different caste and social background, with Heer being of a higher caste and from a wealthier land-owning family, while Ranjha was a buffalo-herder employed by her father. Caught together by the villainous paternal uncle, Kaidho, who walks with a stick for a crutch, due to a withered leg probably from Polio, Heer is first beaten with the stick and then forcibly married to someone of her father's choice. She never gives in and Ranjha takes up a wandering lifestyle, finally turning up at her door, and the two plan to run away again. Her father and uncle trick her, pretending they will give in to her and arrange for a wedding with Ranjha. On the day, however, Kaidho poison's Heer's food, killing her. When Ranjha learns of her death, he also eats some of her food and dies too, being united with her forever in the next world. The story of Heer and Ranjha had been told in the Punjab for a long time, but it was truly immortalised by the poetry of the Sufi poet Waris Shah (1722 to 1798), and is a popular source for modern day cinema.

Baba Bulleh Shah uses the story here and in the second verse says to the Beloved that it is like when you were beating Heer, and battering her with Kaidho's walking stick, you were really beating someone who was already dead to the world and only existed for Ranjha. You ignored her pleas too and tried to silence her, but she did not give up on her love and the two overcame all obstacles in death. Baba Bulleh Shah tells the Beloved that it is no different for him, and that the Beloved can go on and kill him but he will not give up on Him.

In the third verse, Baba Bulleh Shah describes how the Beloved can remain hidden from us, and ways in which people try to bind Him to themselves so He cannot escape. Hindu Brahmin priests used to have their heads clean-shaven, except for a lock of hair at the crown of the head which was allowed to grow. This was a symbol of their devotion to God, in effect God was tied up with them through this lock of hair. A similar visage is presented in Judaism where men do not cut locks of hair on either side of their heads. So, in effect, God keeps trying to be veiled from us, but we find different ways of tying Him to us and not let Him escape or run away.

In the final verse, Baba Bulleh Shah, implores God that You are my Master and I am your slave who is always begging to see Your face. So please now, enough of your games, come and sit deep in my chest, i.e. in my heart.

## 22. The nature of God and man (Rub tay bundhay di zaat).

The nature of God and man is one,

Like the nature of cloth is the fibre,

God is hidden such, within man,

Like fibre is hidden within cloth.


He Himself calls, and Himself answers,

He Himself says "I Am",

If an accomplished Teacher is found, Bullehya,

Then there is no "me" left and no "you"!

The nature of God has interested thinkers from ancient times and people have imagined and depicted God in human form. The mind works in such a way that we understand something better when we can visualise it. Hence, there have been many depictions of gods as statues with human as well as supernatural forms.

The Abrahamic religions teach that God created Man in His own image. This can be interpreted in many ways. It can be interpreted literally by people who may think of God as an old man with a white beard sitting on a throne in Heaven. Another way of interpretation is that when God breathed the spirit into the first man, Adam, He also breathed some of His own nature and qualities into him. Life comes into a person and leaves him only through his spirit or Soul which originated from God. A person is only alive if this spirit is within him and dies as soon as it leaves. Sufis believe that while that spirit which originated from God is within a person, then God through that spirit is with that person. It is this spirit shining through everyone that Baba Bulleh Shah can see and tells him that God accompanies everyone. While the spirit that originated from God is in a person, it is still with God's spirit, so the body it occupies, is also with God. In other words, everything is part of God and God is part of everything. We assign various Natures to God like All-powerful, All-Forgiving, the most Generous, Loving, Kind and many others, which to a lesser extent are also part of human nature too.

In the first verse, Baba Bulleh Shah says that the Natures of God and Man are the same, but it is like fibres that make up a cloth. When we see a cloth, we do not see it's fibres or what makes it a cloth, we see the cloth itself. Just like these fibres cannot be seen in a finished cloth, we also cannot see how God is part of every cell that makes us. God pervades through us to the microscopic level, but we cannot see that, we see the finished human being.

In the second verse, Baba Bulleh Shah, pursues this point further. If God is our fibre to the microscopic levels, and the spirit which originated from God, gives us life, then, Baba Bulleh Shah says, God is part of us, and we part of God. Therefore, when we call out to God, in effect the divine part of us calls out to God, and God answers back telling us "I Am" (Yahweh). This was what he told the Israelites when they called out to him in the wilderness.

Sufis believe that only through an able Murshid can the veils that exist between Man and God be lifted so that we can see that there is no "me" or "you", we are all part of the One.

## 23. White or black (Gori ya kali).

Someone asked a question of Mian Majnu,

Isn't your Laila of a dark complexion?

Mian Majnu answered him thus,

Your eye is not capable of seeing!


The pages of the holy Quran are white,

On them, the writing is with black ink,

Leave it Bullehya, when you have given your heart,

Then what if she's white or she's black!

Baba Bulleh Shah did not believe in discrimination between people based on their religion, caste, colour, race or gender. He saw God in everyone and everything, but unfortunately, society was strictly divided along these lines at the time. The Hindu Caste system was rigid and inflexible and could never be escaped from, even with wealth or education. A person was condemned to being untouchable or unclean (Dalit) for the rest of his life, purely through an accident of birth. Power, religious and secular, was in the hands of higher castes, who guarded the privilege strictly. There may have been a racial element to the caste system too and it is believed that it may have been in place by invading Aryan races from the Caucuses and central Asia. They were of a lighter complexion and finer features then the indigenous people they encountered. In order to preserve their racial purity, they segregated society into castes, an early form of apartheid, disallowing interactions or inter-marriage between them, a form of divide and rule. As Aryan upper castes were distinct with lighter complexions and eye colour, this became more desirable as people formed an idea of someone's caste and standing, simply by their appearance. The darker someone's complexion was, the lower their caste was thought to be. This type of thinking may have left an impression on South Asian society, of all religious backgrounds, even today, with a preference for fairer skin and lighter eyes, especially for women. In this poem, Baba Bulleh Shah tackles these ideas of colour prejudices head-on, using the well-known story of Laila and Majnu.

The saga of Laila and Majnu is an old tale of love from Arabia that may apparently have inspired Shakespeare's Romeo and Juliet. In it the two lovers are from different tribes and backgrounds whose families cannot accept their union. Heartbroken, Majnu, whose real name was Kais, takes to wandering the dessert and crying out for Laila, who also pines for him. In true tragedy-style, the two have to die to be united, suffering hardships and hostility from society. In death, they prove their true love for each other and set an example for others to follow. The term "majnu" is still used to describe someone who is "insane" or has lost his mind.

Baba Bulleh Shah here uses the example of Laila, who was known to be of a dark complexion. In the first verse, someone asks Majnu, in a slightly derogatory manner, that how are you insane with love for a woman who is dark-skinned. Majnu tells him that it is his eyes that are at fault as they are incapable of truly seeing beyond the obvious. To make his point, Baba Bulleh Shah says look at the paper that the Quran is written on. It is white but it only becomes the holy Quran when written on in ink, which is black. It is the black ink which makes the Quran, not the blank white pages. In the same way, when you give your heart to someone, it is not their outer appearance that matters but what is within.

## 24. Wake up (Utth, jaagh)!

Wake up! Stop your snoring,
This slumber is no use for you!

Where now is Alexander the Great?
Death spares not saint nor prophet,
All have left their piles of ruins,
 No-one here is everlasting!

Whatever you do, so you will reap,
Otherwise, you will regret in the end,
Like a lonely crane you will shriek,
For without feathers, there is no flight!

Bulleh! Without the Master there is no-one,
Here, there, in either inn,
Take each step with great care,
For you will not return a second time!

Wake up! Stop your snoring,
This slumber is no use for you!

Baba Bulleh Shah cared deeply for his fellow countrymen and believed in social justice and equality. He was no ordinary Sufi mystic and poet who kept himself confined to spiritual matters but saw peoples' spiritual and physical well-being as interlinked. In order to think higher thoughts and act on a higher plane, people needed to be free from fear and oppression. Only then could they reach their full potential.

At a time when there was no concept of freedom of speech, Baba Bulleh Shah was a revolutionary in his ideas and such despised by the ruling elite and the religious orthodoxy. He was a loud voice of political opposition to the status quo, and they tried to silence him, without success. Baba Bulleh Shah spoke up about gender equality, equal rights of all people regardless of their race, colour, caste or wealth. He called for people not to follow the corrupt religious orthodoxy blindly. He was against domination of one religion over others and generally believed in inclusivity. He wanted to reform society into a more fair and equal footing so that everybody could live in harmony and thrive together. His ideas of social justice were way ahead of his time and would not surface again for another two hundred years.

This poem is almost a rousing, revolutionary call by Baba Bulleh Shah for people to rise up and demand their rights, rather than live in fear and apathy. He tells them that living oppressed lives like this is of no value, as they will never be able to achieve anything. He tells them not to be afraid of their oppressive Rulers, and says no Ruler was ever more powerful than Alexander the Great, but where is he now? Death spares no-one, whether he be Saint or Prophet and no-one is immortal. All come and go, leaving their ruins behind, and so will the current oppressors. They are not to be feared.

Baba Bulleh Shah tells people that whatever they do, so they will reap, and if they do not stand up for themselves, then they will regret it later. This would be like a crane that did not leave with the rest of the flock and is left shrieking in loneliness. It is not possible for one crane to migrate on its own, it needs support from the rest of the flock. In a similar way, people need to rise up together against evil-doers, otherwise they will be left bereft on their own.

In the final verse, Baba Bulleh Shah tells them that only God matters, in this world and the next and people should not fear anyone else.

Baba Bulleh Shah did not believe in re-incarnation and tells people that this is their only chance of life on earth and they should make it worthwhile and live without fear.

## 25. Take out this timekeeper (Khurrhyali daiwo nikaal ni)!

Take out this timekeeper,

My precious sweetheart has come home!

This clock keeps beating second by second,

Thus, shortening this night of our union,

If it could understand my mind's desire,

It would throw away this clock with his own hands!

Take out this timekeeper!

Never-ending, beautiful music is now playing,

The musician, Handsome, and his harmony so perfect,

Forgotten have I fasts, prayers and rituals,

Now, the bartenders are offering goblets of wine!

Take out this timekeeper!

All my sorrow and grief has been lifted,

When I saw His face, it was a wondrous sight,

The night is passing, do something to prolong it,

Put up a wall in-front of the coming day!

Take out this timekeeper!

Bullehya! the Master's abode I adore,

Without being able to swim, I have floated,

So, so rarely has my turn arrived,

That parting now is unbearable!

Take out this timekeeper,

My precious sweetheart has come home!

The Punjabi word "Khurrhi" can have multiple meanings relating to "Time", depending on the context. It can mean "one second" or "one moment" as in "Ik Khurrhi", or to describe a watch. It is gender-based so that a small watch has a female noun "Khurrhi" and a big wall-clock or grandfather clock is called by the male noun "Khurrhyal". Anything that ticks or beats regularly can be described in these terms.

A "Khurrhyali" is the person or object that marks or keeps track of time. For example, on an athletics race track, the "stopwatch" is the "Khurrhi" that ticks second by second and the official in-charge of the stopwatch is the "Khurrhyali", as he is marking time.

In this poem, Baba Bulleh Shah is using both the terms "Khurrhyal" and "Khurrhyali" to describe his heart. It is a "Khurrhyal" as it is behaving like a clock, ticking regularly every second and having its own pattern, but it is also the "Khurrhyali" as its beats also follow and keep track of time.

Sufis place a great emphasis on the heart as the centre for temporal consciousness. They describe many layers and chambers within the heart that become illuminated when we destroy our ego and annihilate the inner self, so that the divine light that is already within us shines through. This is no easy task, and Sufis believe that it cannot be achieved without the help of a learned and able guru (Murshid). Once the Murshid has shown you the way and un-blinkered your eyes, only then can you see God accompanying everyone as Baba Bulleh Shah says.

By placing the site of spiritual awakening in the heart, Sufis are not denying that the brain is the centre for the control of bodily senses and functions, but as Baba Bulleh Shah says in many of his poems that when you find the divine light and spiritual enlightenment, then all rhyme and reason goes out of the window. Our sense of reality is lost, and we experience a sense of being that cannot be measured or quantified by use of those senses.

Sufis use the term "heart" loosely in this respect and understand that this centre of divine light within us may not physically be the organ we call the heart, but an area close to it within our chest that contains our spirit or soul. Whatever or wherever that point of light is within us, we can use the "heart" as its metaphor.

With the advancement of scientific knowledge about the workings of the human body, Western thought made the brain the pivotal organ for human life and knowledge and relegated the heart to the role of a mere pump for moving blood around the body. The brain does control our body functions and senses, but this does not explain all the experiences and feelings a person may have. A person with a damaged brain, as in a persistent vegetative state, can be kept alive for many years on a ventilator, as long as the heart is working. The same cannot be done for someone whose heart has totally stopped or been damaged. The heart muscle, once injured or destroyed, can never recover or regenerate unlike other muscles in the body.

The Sufi way to think, then, is that there is within us a place where our divine spirit resides and this place is metaphorically the heart. This spirit that differentiates between life and death, was breathed into the first man, Adam, by God, and has subsequently been dividing exponentially millions of times. So, in each person, there is a segment of that original spirit that God placed in Adam, hence in each person there is a divine part of God. Although God is within each of us, He is veiled from us, and we do not see Him. To be able to see God in ourselves and in others, this veil has to be removed. Only then can we see God everywhere. In some people, it is easy to recognise the presence of God, by their behaviours and actions which has made the veil between them and God much thinner. In other people who are following their ego and worldly desires, the veil is much thicker and it may not be so easy to see God within them, although He is still there, through that original divine spirit.

Baba Bulleh Shah worked his entire life to destroy his inner ego and to lift the veil between himself and God, with the help of his Murshid, Shah Innayat. In this poem, he describes the feeling and fulfilment of longing when he finally achieves this and experiences the presence of God in his heart. He lays out the poem in the form of fulfilment of love that a woman might feel when she is finally in the arms of her beloved, and all her desires are finally fulfilled, as may happen on her wedding night. The feeling of fulfilment may be so strong that she does not want time to pass or the night to end, and she would do anything to stop this happening. She sees that the beats of her heart are beating time, and the timekeeper in her heart is marking time, so she asks that this timekeeper is taken out of her or expelled because her precious beloved has finally come into her heart and she does not want time with him to end.

In the first verse, Baba Bulleh Shah, describes this anxiety she is experiencing as she has no control over her heart, beating second by second and with each beat the time and the night passing, leaving less and less of the night together. She says if only the heart could understand her mind's desire for the night not to pass, then, it would throw itself out, and stop time forever.

In effect, Baba Bulleh Shah is saying that now that God has finally entered his heart, he wishes, his heart would stop beating, i.e. he could die in this state of rapture with God.

In the second verse, Baba Bulleh Shah describes those feelings of rapture by using the state of bliss that Muslims hope to experience in Paradise. These depictions of Paradise come from the Quran, and describe the place where all good Muslims hope to go for eternity, after the Day of Judgement, if they have lived good lives.

Baba Bulleh Shah describes this feeling as though already in Paradise, now that God has come into him. He says it is like never-ending gentle music is being played by beautiful angelic beings. The music is like he has never heard before and is perfect to his ears. He now, no longer needs to worry about fasting, prayers or any other Muslim rituals, and all his wishes are fulfilled. Drinking wine, which is forbidden to Muslims in this world, will not be so in the next, and those in Paradise will be able to drink to their heart's content without suffering any ill effects. The cherubic bartenders will fill your glass to the brim without being asked.

In Paradise, there will be no grief or sorrow, but people will be in a state of bliss and rapture living in God's light for eternity. Here on earth, on Baba Bulleh Shah's night of union with the Beloved, the time and night are passing, and he pleads for something to be done to prolong it. If only a wall could be built in front of the fast-approaching day.

In the final verse, Baba Bulleh Shah tells us that he loves this state of rapture and being with the Beloved and does not know how he was lucky enough to have experienced it. He then uses the metaphor of a polygamous Muslim marriage where the husband is obliged to spend equal time with each of his wives and to go to them in rotation. Muslim Law allows four wives per man, but Emperors and Sultans may circumvent this by having numerous concubines. A wife may have to wait years before it is her turn to see her husband again. Each day without him has been a burden for her and now that it is her turn, she does not want to let go of him. Even the thought of him leaving is so difficult for her that she wishes she passes in this state of union with him.

## 26. Difficult (Okha)!

Fool..., to earn true love is difficult!

Making someone your true friend is difficult!

Love, love, everyone bellows,

Having loved, fulfilling it is difficult!


Anyone can laugh at others' misfortunes,

Sharing someone's sorrow is difficult!

Words alone do not gain a Sufi's station,

Changing into a wanderer's guise is difficult!


Bullehya! no one listens to what someone says,

Making people understand is difficult!

This poem is about the difficulties that confront you, on the Sufi path.

In Punjabi, "ishq" means true love, or being passionately in love with someone. This love can be human or divine, as in the case of Sufis who see God as embodiment of "True Love" and are also passionately in love with Him. In the first two lines, Baba Bulleh Shah explains the difficulty in obtaining true love and making someone your true friend (Yaar). He says that everyone goes on about love and being in love, but the difficulty is not falling in love but then honouring that true love.

In the second verse, Baba Bulleh Shah says that it is easy for people to laugh at others' misfortunes, but not easy to share their burden.

"Rutbay" means honours or titles. Sufis progress through arduous stages in their training from their "Murshid". They have to work extremely hard to reach each of these stages of learning and it can many years to even reach the lowest rung.

"Jogi" in Punjabi relates to a person gives up everything in the way of God and subsists from day to day with whatever he is given in the way of food, giving blessings in return. Such men typically did not stay in one place for long, wandering from village to village, calling out for alms and food. They only owned what they carried with them. They wore a long, rough, loose-fitting robe "Cholla", often of saffron, green or red depending on the Sufi order they belonged to. This was often repaired and covered in patches of different coloured materials. On their heads would be a large turban to protect against the sun and on their shoulders, they carried a thick sack-cloth, woollen blanket (Loi) that they pulled over themselves when they slept. In their hand they would have a long wooden staff to protect themselves against danger from wild animals. Sometimes the staff would have a small bell attached to it that would ring as they went, letting people know they were coming so they would come out to give them any offerings of food or money.

The "jogis" (Yogi) wear a single earring (Mundri) in one ear and a single ring on one finger. Around their necks would be a bead necklace (Gaani). Under their shoulder would be tucked away a begging bowel (Kashkol), into which people would place any offerings of food if they had spare. The basic "kashkol" would have been carved out of wood in a boat-like fashion with a cloth or chain tied to each end that could be draped over the shoulder. Any food they gathered, they would then go and eat and share amongst other companions. This was the typical guise of the "jogi" and this was all he owned. Baba Bulleh Shah says that people do not just attain Sufi wisdom, even changing into this "jogi" guise, giving up all that you own is difficult for most people.

In the final couplet, Baba Bulleh Shah bemoans that people do not listen to advice or pay heed to wisdom and prefer to do their own thing. He says making these people understand is difficult.

## 27. Birds (Punchi).

Consider o man, the birds flying in the sky,

Just reflect on what they do.

Neither do they hoard food,

Nor do they die of hunger!


Has anyone ever seen,

These winged creatures starving to death?

Only mankind hoards food,

And it is people who die of starvation!

When God created man and breathed life into him, He crucially endowed him with something that set him apart from angels, and all other creatures on earth: free will. Under Islamic thinking, this free will was to be the trial for each person, by which they would be reckoned on the Day of Judgement. If they chose God and stood with good while rejecting evil, they would be rewarded with everlasting bliss in Paradise. If they rejected God and did mischief on earth, they would be condemned to everlasting torture in Hell.

All other creatures that adorn the earth were denied this free will and are not able to pick and choose their destinies, and neither will they be judged on their actions on earth. God has set a path for all these creatures, and they follow those paths without question.

This complete submission to the will of God by all creatures other than man has always been envied by spiritual beings who long to emulate this total trust in God without their egos pushing them towards self-gratification. Thinkers and Prophets have used examples of behaviours of birds and animals to highlight how these creatures survive and thrive with the help of God, without resorting to wars and violence and all the other evils that man resorts to for wealth and power.

Blessed and holy people spend their lives trying to achieve a state where they expel this given free will, and live without the cares of the short-term delights of this world. In the Bible, Jesus says: Look at the birds of the air: they neither sow nor reap or harvest and yet your Lord God feeds them.

In this poem, Baba Bulleh Shah uses a similar analogy to highlight a curse which afflicted Punjab then, and still haunts many countries of South Asia and elsewhere; namely, hoarding!

Hoarding, particularly of foodstuffs and commodities is often used by wealthy merchants and powerful criminal groups to create an artificial situation of scarcity in order to inflate prices and make big profits. Typically, non-perishable food stuffs such as rice, grain, pulses, flour, sugar, oil, will be purchased in vast quantities at cheap rates and disappeared into huge stores, making them unavailable to market. This relative scarcity causes panic and inflates prices sky high making a huge profit for these unscrupulous people. Such practices increase at times of strife and weak governments as was the case during the lifetime of Baba Bulleh Shah, resulting in famines and starvation. Many infamous famines have been known to have occurred at a time of plenty, purely through the hoarding and disappearance of foods by avaricious men.

## 28. Faith in One God (Tawheed).

Being learned, does not make noble,

Those who are genuinely base,

Brass can never become gold,

Even if we set it with rubies and diamonds!


A miser can never give alms,

Though he has millions in treasure,

Bullehya! without faith in one God, Paradise will not be gained,

Even if we were to die in holy Medina!

"Tawheed" is of Arabic origin and literally means "Union" or Unity of One. In Islam, it denotes the Oneness, or Unity of God, as opposed to god in many forms. Islam teaches that there is only One true God, Allah, and nothing else can be associated with Him.

The other Abrahamic religions such as Judaism and Christianity also assert the Oneness of God.

For Sufis, who can relate to many pathways leading to finding God, and who respect all Faiths, there is no compromise on the Unity of God.

In this poem, Baba Bulleh Shah uses examples of things that are impossible and asserts to Muslims that just like these things, unless you believe in One God, you will not enter Paradise even if you died in the holy city of Medina in Arabia, the second holiest site in Islam.

The Oneness of God is crucial to beliefs of Sufis as they believe that it is this One True God that pervades everything in the whole Universe.

## 29. I am without confines (Main bay-kaidh)!

I am without confines, I am without bounds,

                Neither am I afflicted, nor am I the healer!

Not am I a Believer, nor am I a heathen,

                Neither am I a Sayyid, nor am I a commoner!

By fourteen generations are we descended,

                Nowhere can we be confined!

In the lowly is our life,

                In that, there is no doubt nor fault!

Why do you ask the caste of Bulleh Shah?

                It neither exists, nor is desirable!

I am without confines; I am without bounds!

It is not hard to believe the impact Baba Bulleh Shah had during his own lifetime. Not only was he a Sufi mystic and poet but he believed in social justice. He always spoke the truth, no matter how unpalatable for some and tried to wake people up and to stand up for their rights to security and equality. No wonder followers and foes were all asking about who he was, where he had come from, what was his caste and what was his agenda.

Baba Bulleh Shah was of Muslim birth and a "Sayyid", descended from the family of the Prophet Muhammed (Peace be upon him). This set him in a high rank within Muslims, but Baba Bulleh Shah rejected notions of caste on the basis of birth alone. His ideas differed from the religious orthodoxy of the time so greatly that they tried to expel him from the ranks of Muslims. Even on his death, Muslim Clerics (Mullans) refused to lead his funeral prayers and he was not allowed to be buried in a Muslim cemetery.

Baba Bulleh Shah was very much aware of the questions being asked about him, and in this poem, he addresses them by saying of himself that he is without confines and cannot be categorized in any way, in terms of his outlook. He tells them that neither is he mad and nor does he claim to be a healer. They can see him as a Believer or a heathen, and neither is he a "Sayyid" nor any other caste. He confirms that he is descended from the family of the Prophet (Peace be upon him) by fourteen generations, but that he is not going to be confined to anything on the basis of this. He says that he sees himself being lowly and amongst the lowliest is his life, he says there is no shame in being such.

Baba Bulleh Shah was irritated by people asking his caste and talking about his lifestyle amongst the poorest and rejects of society, while being a Sayyid. He rejected these notions and tells them to stop asking about his caste. He says I have no caste and neither does he desire to belong to one.

## 30. Ranjha, Ranjha (Ranjha, Ranjha).

Chanting Ranjha, Ranjha, now I have myself become Ranjha,

Forever now, see me as Ranjha, no one call me Heer!

Ranjha is within me, I am within Ranjha, no other thoughts occur to us,

There is no me, it is all Him, this is how He amuses Himself.

Whatever shows from within us, that is our nature,

 One with whom I have become enamoured, I have become like him.

Take off the white shawl o' maiden, put on the wanderers' cloak,

The white shawl will become stained, the black cloak shows no stains.

Take me to Takht Huzaray Bullehya, in Syal I find no peace,

Chanting Ranjha, Ranjha, now I have myself become Ranjha.

In this poem Baba Bulleh Shah uses the story of Heer and Ranjha to convey two important concepts; unrequited love and the idea of chanting the name and wanting someone so much that you become that person yourself.

Heer from Syal and Ranjha from Takht Huzara feature in a tragic Punjabi love story where the two lovers are prevented from getting married, due to different castes and social standing. Heer's father first forces her to marry someone else, which leads to Ranjha taking to wandering the countryside, calling out for her. When Heer refuses to compromise and accept her forced marriage, her family trick her that she will be allowed to marry Ranjha but is poisoned by her paternal uncle Kaidho, on the wedding day. Ranjha, realising what has happened, also eats the poisoned food and dies with Heer.

This love story was turned into an epic poem by the Sufi poet, Waris Shah (1722-1798) who used it as a metaphor of unrequited love between man and the divine, and is still recited today. In this he portrays man, wandering and searching for the divine, chanting His name, but not attaining Him. Here Baba Bulleh Shah uses the same concepts to highlight man's search for God.

Ritual chanting of God's name is an ancient custom that brings strength and protection to one who is chanting. In Islam, it is called "Zikr" and refers to chanting "Allah" repeatedly, the rhythm starting slowly but then picking up gradually to a crescendo, inducing a state of trance.

The aim of chanting the name of someone, or, for example "Alif" for Allah, is first to have that entity at the front of your thoughts and to eliminate all other chatter that might be happening in your brain. Secondly, it allows you to focus on that name you are chanting and on all its attributes. Once secondary chatter has been cleared out and you are focused on the One, then you behave like the One would want you to behave, as He is there at the front of your mind. Hence, focussing on and repeating the name of the One constantly brings you closer and closer to Him. If this analogy is pushed to the ultimate, that if you think of someone and chant their name constantly and want to be with them so much that no other thought comes to mind, then it is almost as though your reason for existing, is that desire that you are yearning for. One must not look at this from a point of view of an obsession with someone or something which is to do with control over something, but look at it from point of view of desiring something and loving something so much that you want to be a part of them. Hence by chanting the name of God and desiring God to be within you, and you to be part of God, is the ultimate aim.

In the first line of the poem, this is exactly what Heer is describing. She is chanting "Ranjha, Ranhja" and thinking of him and desiring to be with him so much that she, in effect has become Ranjha. She tells people not to call her Heer anymore but to see her as a manifestation of Ranjha himself. The same is the situation for Ranjha who is constantly chanting "Heer". In effect the two only exist in each other and for each other, and entertain no other concerns.

The fourth line is the Sufi concept that God is in everything and in everyone. So, the Divine is in Heer and it is also in Ranjha, i.e., God is in both. Although God is in both, Heer and Ranjha are apart. So, Heer says there is no me, i.e., she as Heer is irrelevant and Ranjha as Ranjha is irrelevant, it is the divine within them that matters, and it is He who is just amusing Himself, by playing these games with Himself.

Baba Bulleh Shah rejected notions of discrimination based on caste or colour and in line five Heer says what shows through from inside us is our true nature, not the man-made differences. Her nature has become one with Ranjha, so now he shines through her and she has become him.

In lines seven and eight, Baba Bulleh Shah tells us that worldly constraints and differences based on high and low, are designed to restrict and control our natures by creating notions of honour and class. Living in such a society requires conformity and stepping outside of its boundaries puts a stain on your character. By becoming a Sufi, however, you let go of all those prejudices and see things with a different light, where there are no such constraints.

In line nine, Heer says take me to Takht Huzara, Bullehya as I find no peace in Syal. In other words, take me to the land of my beloved Ranjha as there is no peace for me here. In Sufi terms, take me to be with God, as there is no peace for me here on earth.

## 31. Haji folk (Haji Lok).

Haji folk go to Mecca,

My soulmate Ranjha is my Mecca,

                O I'm a fool!

I am betrothed to my love Ranjha,

But my father is trying to deceive me,

                O I'm a fool!

Haji folk go to Mecca,

In my heart are nine hundred Meccas,

                O I'm a fool!

Amongst them are Hajis, amongst them Qazis,

Amongst them are thieves and tricksters,

                O I'm a fool!

Haji folk go to Mecca,

We will go to Takht Huzara,

                O I'm a fool!

Whichever direction is the Beloved, that way is the Kaaba,

Even if you search through the four Holy Books!

                O I'm a fool!

"Haji" is a title given to Muslims who perform the Hajj Pilgrimage to Mecca in Arabia. Hajj is one of the five pillars of Islam and is obligatory on adult Muslims who are physically and financially able to perform it, at least once during their lifetime. It is performed during a set time of the year only, and involves performing various rites in and around Mecca. The pinnacle of these is circumambulation of the Kaaba, a cube shaped sanctuary at the centre of the Holy Mosque, Haram e Sharif, believed to have been built by the prophet Abraham as a House of God. Hajj is a way for Muslims to link with God, offering true repentance and seeking forgiveness for past sins. Muslims who have achieved this honour are held in great esteem by the community as they are committing to living a more pious life. Along with the respect and esteem that a Haji receives is the risk that some people will undertake it to gain this standing in the community, rather than its true purpose. This is something that many Sufi Saints pointed out in their poetry. It would not have been easy to criticise such upstanding people who have been to Hajj, so the poets had to be mindful of this, and in this poem Baba Bulleh Shah again speaks through Heer to say, "But, O I'm a fool" or you can call me a fool. It can also be read as look at all these things I am telling you like, my true love for Ranjha, that we feel divinely betrothed to each other, that my father is ignoring this and trying to trick me into accepting something else. She asks them what wrong is she doing if all she cares and thinks about is Ranjha and wants to be with him, does she not have a choice or the right to choose for herself? She tells them you can call me a fool but this what she believes!

In the first two lines, Baba Bulleh Shah says, through Heer, that people turn to Mecca and go and perform the Hajj there, as their ultimate goal to find the divine, but to her, her beloved Ranjha is the focal point. But, she admits, O I'm a fool.

Heer then says that she knows her soul was betrothed to Ranjha, when they were both created, but now her father is trying to trick her. Again, she says O I am a fool!

People may go to Mecca to perform the Hajj once, but Heer says, in her heart are the equivalent of nine hundred Meccas where she is constantly performing the hajj of her beloved Ranjha.

The Hajj is performed by Muslims from all over the world and of all backgrounds. In lines seven and eight, Heer says that performing the Hajj will be Muslims,

Qazis (Muslim judges), as well as thieves and tricksters and rogues of all types. She compares this to her own one true soul, performing hajj for Ranjha in her heart. She then says that unlike people heading to Mecca, she would prefer to go to Ranjha's homeland of Takht Huzara, to be with her true love.

The four holy books referred to in the last two lines are the Torah, the Psalms of King David, the New Testament and the Quran. These are deemed to be divine holy books in Islam and their followers are referred to as "The People of the Book". Baba Bulleh Shah is saying that all these four holy books point to the same fact that God is in everything, in everyone and everywhere. Though Hajis go to Mecca and Muslims pray in the direction of the Kaaba in Mecca, Heer says that she can see God in all directions, and for her whatever direction her beloved Ranjha is in, that is the focal point for her devotions. But she concludes, but of course, I'm but a fool!

## 32. Such perverse times have come (Ultay hor zumaanay ayai).

Such perverse times have come,

That I have been able to learn the secrets of the Beloved.


Crows have started killing falcons, and sparrows have downed hawks,

Horses graze from rubbish heaps, and donkeys are being fed horseweed.


There is no love between relations, whether be maternal or paternal uncles,

No unity between father and sons, or with daughters, their mothers.


Honest people are getting pushed away, while liars are being sat close,

The heirs have been bankrupted; the followers are now holding court.


Sackcloth-wearers have been made Rajahs, the Rajahs made to beg,

Bullehya! the order has come from the Supreme, who can turn this away?


Such perverse times have come,

That I have been able to learn the secrets of the Beloved.

Baba Bulleh Shah believed strongly in social justice. As has been described above, Punjab, during his lifetime, was going through very turbulent times. After the death of the Mughal Emperor Aurangzeb Alamgir (1618-1707), the Mughal Empire had started to slowly decline, and law and order started to break down. The Sikhs were waging guerrilla warfare for their survival and pursuit of sovereignty, against corrupt and blood-thirsty officials. Bribery and nepotism were rife and the ordinary man was greatly oppressed, at their hands. Baba Bulleh Shah was greatly aggrieved at the state of affairs, and in this poem describes the detrimental changes he is seeing in society, interpreting it in the light of the divine hand bringing about the changes, that these petty despots cannot stop. He says that such upside down, topsy-turvy and unpredictable times have come, that it has made him see some of the mysterious ways in which the Divine moves.

In line three, Baba Bulleh Shah talks about the changing times almost breaking laws of nature, such as the crows starting to kill falcons, and sparrows downing hawks. People who would normally prize and look after their horses, feeding them on prime feeds are no longer able to do so and those who could only afford donkeys are now able to feed them rich horseweed. Using these metaphors, Baba Bulleh Shah is actually talking about the ruling classes and Governors of Punjab where mighty Mughal armies are being defeated by small numbers of organised Sikhs of the Khalsa movement. The rulers who should be nourishing the honest and the capable are instead promoting the weak and corrupt sycophants, hastening their own demise.

Baba Bulleh Shah then describes the breakdown in the fabric of society where there is no longer love or affection between relations and everyone is out for themselves.

Honest people applying for jobs and promotions are being kicked away, and instead the liars and corrupt raised up on receipt of large bribes or connections. The chosen heirs of these privileged people are suddenly being thrown out, and instead, opportunities mean that the previous menials and low-ranked are now holding court.

In line nine, Baba Bulleh Shah mentions "Sackcloth-wearers" being made Rajahs and Rajahs being made to beg. By this he means ordinary people of little means from the countryside taking control and becoming rulers themselves forcing the previous masters into destitution. This is sometimes interpreted as the rise of the Sikh Khalsa movement, which had its roots in the poor of the countryside, and their success in deposing Mughal officials, who would have been more used to wearing silks and brocade rather than poor garments.

Ultimately, Baba Bulleh Shah says that all these changes are at the behest of the divine and that His orders cannot be put off. In these changes however, he can see what the divine is doing in the movements that are starting to bring down a corrupt system.

## 33. Now, who are You hiding Yourself from (Hunh kiss thinh)?

Somewhere you teach Sunnah and religious obligations, somewhere you are the Mullan, saying the call to prayer,

Somewhere you are professing Ram, somewhere you are applying the tilak-mark to your forehead,

Now, who are You hiding yourself from?

Somewhere you are a thief, somewhere the Qazi, somewhere you climb the pulpit and give sermons,

Somewhere you are Tegh Bahadur Ghazi, upon yourself, charging an army,

Now, who are you hiding yourself from?

You adopt many different guises, the wine You keep all to Yourself,

To me, You are visible everywhere, You Yourself are carrying it all,

Now, who are you hiding yourself from?

The one who searches for You, he is dead before dying,

Even in death he is afraid of You, the dead are never brought back,

Now, who are you hiding yourself from?

"Consciousness", is it mine or is it Yours? In the end it is a mound of dust,

This mound of dust my Beloved has surrounded, this pile of dust is being made to perform,

Now, who are You hiding yourself from?

Bullah! now you really understand the Master, you can recognise Him by His guises,

Somewhere You are coming, somewhere You are going, now I will not be able to lose You,

Now, who are you hiding yourself from?

When Baba Bulleh Shah had his eyes truly opened by his Murshid, Shah Inaayat, and began to see God in everything and accompanying everyone, he learnt that God could no longer hide from him. He now knew all the guises (Rumzanh), the divine employed to remain hidden, and these no longer worked on Baba Bulleh Shah. In this poem, he says to the Almighty, now who are You hiding Yourself from, almost like "who are You Kidding?". He then lists the different ways the divine causes confusion in people's mind as to who He is, in-order to remain veiled from us, but tells Him these are no longer going to work on him as he can now recognise Him anywhere.

Muslim law is based on two main fundamentals; Farz, religious obligations ordered by God in the holy Quran and Sunnat, the examples set by the holy Prophet Muhammed (peace be upon him), as to how he lived his life.

Thus, in the first two lines, Baba Bulleh Shah is saying that somewhere God is to be seen in the guise of a Muslim Scholar teaching people about religion, what is "Sunnat" and "Farz", and somewhere He may appear as a lowly "Mullan", simple cleric, leading prayers in a village mosque.

In the third and fourth lines he uses "professing Ram" to mean a Hindu priest, and the "tilak" mark is the red vermillion mark that a Hindu priest applies to his own and worshippers' foreheads. Hence Baba Bulleh Shah is saying that he can see the divine in each of these different guises, and who does He now think He is hiding Himself from?

In line six and seven, Baba Bulleh Shah says that somewhere the divine shines through a thief, maybe one who steals from the rich to give to the poor, and somewhere in a just "Qazi", Muslim Judge. Somewhere else He may show in an imam, or Muslim religious leader.

Guru Tegh Bahadur Ji was the ninth Guru of the Sikhs, who was martyred by the Mughal Emperor Aurangzeb Alamgir, five years before Baba Bulleh Shah was born. He was an incredible swordsman and was unmatched in his bravery on the battlefield. In line eight, Baba Bulleh Shah declares him a "Ghazi", a title usually reserved for Muslim holy warriors who distinguish themselves on the battlefield when fighting in the way of God. So, with this one line, Baba Bulleh Shah incurred the wrath of the Muslim establishment and religious orthodoxy by firstly honouring a Sikh as a Ghazi and implying that he was fighting in the way of God, even though he was fighting against Muslim Mughals. Secondly, Baba Bulleh Shah, instead of using a general term like before of Qazi or Mullan, actually uses the name of Guru Tegh Bahadur Ji as a person he sees the divine shining through and again asks Him, now who are You hiding Yourself from?

In lines thirteen and fourteen, Baba Bulleh Shah, describes how those who search for God are virtually dead in this life because they think of nothing else but Him. Their whole time and energy are devoted to searching for the divine and then holding onto Him. They have no cares for the world and are yet afraid of what will await them on death because no-one who dies, ever comes back to tell us what it is like. Here, Baba Bulleh Shah is really talking about his own life spent in search of God before he was able to see Him, and he is also speaking about his own mortality.

What sets humans apart from animals is our self-awareness. How did we get this and where did it come from? Why do other living creatures not have this ability? In theological terms, this consciousness has come from God who breathed life into the first human being, Adam. Hence in lines sixteen and seventeen, Baba Bulleh Shah questions this and asks is this awareness through which we have the ability to choose right and wrong, is it truly ours or is it part of the divine; in effect do we really have free choice or is it something that is really God's and He uses it to make this perishable body of clay dance to His tune?

In the final verse, Baba Bulleh Shah sums up by stating that he now truly understands the nature of God and can recognise Him by His actions in whatever guise He may be in. He says that now he has learnt this lesson, he will not let the divine evade him again or hide from him.

## 34. They Came to persuade Bulleh (Bulleh noon sumjhavan).

They came to persuade Bulleh, his sisters and sisters-in-law.

"Accept o' Bullehya, what we say, let go associating with Arrains,

On the line of the Prophet, and decedents of Ali, why have you brought shame?"

"Whosoever sees us as a Sayyid, shall be punished in hell,

Whoever calls us an Arrain, shall frolic in paradise!"

Arrains, wandering beggars, all have their place, God does not differentiate,

Like those who shun the prettiest, and hold dear the unattractive.

If you are looking for blooming gardens, become a follower of the Arrains,

Why are you asking of Bulleh Shah's caste? Be thankful for his choices.

Baba Bulleh Shah wrote this poem to outline where women from his family, including sisters and sisters-in-law, came to see him and tried to get him to give up his association with his Murshid, Shah Inaayat, who was of the farming, Arrain caste as compared to Bulleh Shah's much higher Sayyid background.

The women tell Bulleh Shah to heed them and to not bring shame on the line of the Prophet (peace be upon him) and descendants of Ali by associating with a lower caste.

Baba Bulleh Shah abhorred differences based on race, colour, creed and gender and he rejected the caste system outright, saying that what shines from within someone is their true caste. He was, therefore, unhappy to be told to uphold his superiority based on being a descendent of the holy family and tells the women that those who see him as a "Sayyid" shall be punished in Hell and those who disregard this distinction shall enter Heaven.

Baba Bulleh Shah tells the women, that no matter of what background or caste, everyone has their place and that God does not discriminate between people. He gives them the example of someone who might love someone who is otherwise seen as ugly but would not swap her for anyone else. Whether this was a comment on one of the haranguing women, is for the reader to decide!

Shah Inaayat, Baba Bulleh Shah's Murshid belonged to the Arrain caste and was employed as the gardener at the Shalimar Gardens in Lahore. In the final two lines, Baba Bulleh Shah tells the women that if you like plants and beautiful gardens, then follow Arrains and stop pestering him about caste. Just be grateful for who he has chosen to follow.

## 35. Show me your abode (Upranh dhus tikaana).

Show me your abode, where did you come from, and where will you go?

The wealth on which you pride yourself,

That will not go with you!

You oppress and torment people,

You have taken the job of feeding off loot.

Wag your tail for these four days,

In the end you will be gone!

You will take your abode in the city of the silent,

Where the world will be confined.

By the armfuls, he takes across the powerful,

The expert angel of death,

Compared to all the ones here, O Bullehya,

He is an ancient professional!

Show me your abode, where did you come from, and where will you go?

The opening line of this poem asks people to recognise the reality of their short lives on earth and to recognise that their true abode is the ground in which they will be buried. It is addressed to all, but particularly to the rich and powerful Muslim rulers of the time, as it talks about wealth, power and burial rather than cremation practiced by other religions.

It is certainly possible that Baba Bulleh Shah had the powerful Mughal General/Governor, Mirza Askari (1635-1710), better known by his official title of Wazir Khan, in mind when he wrote this poem.

Wazir Khan was the Faujdar, the military commander of Mughal forces based at the heavily fortified, second city of Punjab, located midway between Dilli (Delhi) and Lahore, named Sirhind. He was zealous in trying to destroy the Sikhs and fought many wars with their tenth Guru, Guru Gobind Singh. In 1704, he treacherously captured the two youngest sons of Guru Gobind Singh, Sahbzada Fateh Singh, nine years, and Sahbzada Zorawer Singh, who was only six years old, and ordered them to be killed by being bricked alive inside a castle wall.

Baba Bulleh Shah did not believe that any person should be persecuted or killed on the basis of their race, religion, gender or caste, so he saw the killing of two innocent children in this way, as a crime against humanity. Baba Bulleh Shah thought very highly of Guru Gobind Singh Ji and had likely been in touch with him, personally or through letters, and was dismayed at his loss. Bloodthirsty rulers and generals were not uncommon at the time, but the killing of two innocent children in such a horrible way took things to a new low.

In the poem, Baba Bulleh Shah says that the wealth you take pride in is not going to go with you at the end. He says, you oppress and torment people and have turned living off their loot as your duty. Wag your tail for these few days you have but, in the end, you will be gone.

The cemetery is often described as "Sher-e-khamoshan" or the city of the silent (Dead). Baba Bulleh Shah says, you will go and take your abode in the city of the silent, where your entire world would be just your grave. Muslims believe that death occurs when the angel of death (Mulk-ul-maut), Azrael, takes one's life. Baba Bulleh Shah says that this Angel of death takes lives thousands at a time and says that these petty, bloodthirsty men who think they are so powerful, have nothing in comparison to him. The poem is a reminder to these wicked men that they will not succeed, whatever heinous acts they perform.

## 36. True Love (Ishq).

I entered the Ministry of True Love,

Thereafter, True Love took away my understanding,

I had gone to get acclaim from True Love,

Thereafter, True Love took away my reasoning.


True Love robs Messengers and Prophets,

It has stolen many kingdoms from their kings,

What has been stolen from you yet Bullehya?

This True Love has stolen God's whole creation!

True Love (Ishq), refers to the natural bond that exists between God and man, whereby God loves His creation, man, and the true nature of man is to love God. In this poem, Baba Bulleh Shah uses the analogy of God the Creator being the Ruler and having various Ministries under Him. The Ministry in this case is of Spirituality or Sufiism. Baba Bulleh Shah describes how when he entered into this Ministry and saw the Truth, he lost all his previous learning and understanding, such was the power of this Truth. It was as if everything he had ever learnt, no longer made sense to him at all. He thought he was going to be rewarded by True Love for entering His Ministry but instead, it took away his reasoning and knowledge so that all the rituals and rules no longer made sense.

Baba Bulleh Shah says that this is how True Love affects Messengers and Prophets, and others, by showing them His Love so that they no longer care for any worldly desires and set off on the path of truth. In the second line of the second verse, he references Sidarrtha Gautam, who was a prince, but gave up his Kingdom to search for enlightenment and became the Buddha.

Finally, Baba Bulleh Shah laughs at himself saying that what has been stolen from you yet Bullehya, True Love has even encompassed God's own Godliness in His love for His creation.

## 37. Ego (Nafs).

Chanting God, God, have become old, mullans and pandits all,

They found no trace of God, becoming weary of their prostrations!

But God resides within you, in the Quran are signs,

Bulleh Shah, God will be found by him, who kills his own ego!

Sufis were aware of the destructive aspects of the "Ego" long before Sigmund Freud (1850–1939) described it. They saw a dichotomy within man, where a part of the spirit which God had breathed into Adam, the essence, was always turned to God and yearning to be reunited with Him. The other part, "Nafs" or the ego was that which is placed within us to enable us to survive in this earthly world that we are placed in for a time, and this focuses on the worldly desires and comforts. It is this ego that keeps our spiritual side, and God, veiled from us. The more a person gives in to his ego, the more veiled God becomes in him and difficult to see. When the ego is controlled or ultimately destroyed, the veil hiding God within man falls and God can be seen shining through him.

The ego is extremely powerful, as it needs to be for us to survive in some very adverse circumstances. It also has the ability to mislead us by constantly whispering to us to satisfy our urges. At other times it may deceive us that we are doing work in God's way but in reality, it is for our own gain. Sufis try to counteract these deceptions by placing their trust and ego in the supervision of a Murshid who then monitors and corrects any such aberrations and illusions.

In the first two lines of this Kafi (quatrain), Baba Bulleh Shah points to the futility of Muslim clerics and Hindu priests, growing old, performing ritual prayers (Namaz) and chanting "Ram, Ram", and feeling frustrated that they cannot find any sign of Him.

Baba Bulleh Shah then says that God is within us and there are signs pertaining to this in all the holy books. In the Quran, for example, God says that He is closer to us than our own carotid artery, the vital blood vessel in the neck carrying blood from the heart to the brain.

If God is so close and within us, then how is it that we do not see Him? What can we do to see Him? Baba Bulleh Shah tells us that this can only happen when we destroy our own ego and focus more on our inner essence that is part of God. People who can do this, will be the ones to find God, not the ones doing mere rituals without intent.

## 38. Friend (Yaar).

The friend who has a thousand friends,

Don't consider that friend a friend,

He who loves you beyond limits,

Don't consider that love as love.


He is a friend, and causes you a loss,

Don't consider that loss a loss,

Bulleh Shah, no matter how poor your friend may be,

Don't consider his fellowship as worthless!

People, on the whole, tend to make friendships with others either of their own station or above, and rarely does a powerful man have a poor fellow as a friend. Social divides are as marked today as they were 400 years ago and the gap between rich and poor is no less either. This poem seems to have been written for today's society that places such emphasis on social media and aspirations for celebrity.

We all know people who appear to be surrounded by "friends" all the time appearing to have the time of their lives. Baba Bulleh Shah says that don't consider such a friend a friend because he will not be there when you need him. True friendships are few and true friends are hard to find. The friend who has a thousand friends is an acquaintance and not a friend. This is something that also applies to online friends and followers. Some people will have thousands of these and not a single true friend they can talk to. Hence loneliness is one of the biggest factors causing stress and mental health problems in the young who live for "likes" on their social media posts.

Someone who loves you beyond limits is not showing love but obsession. Baba Bulleh Shah says do not consider this type of overwhelming attachment as love but to be weary of it as it leads to control and smothers the target.

If you have a true friend, then you have to value and cherish them and stand by them, even if it causes you discomfort in terms of your social standing or other dealings. Finally, Baba Bulleh Shah says that poverty has nothing to do with the worth of a person, and should never be a factor in choosing friends. A true friend, no matter how poor is worth their weight in gold.

## 39. This True Love (Ais Ishq).

This True Love has a strange tradition,

It robs you in the meeting of an eye,

People make others enemies, to rob them,

But this robs you by making you a friend!


Where True Love has barely glimpsed,

There, wisdom has lost all reasoning,

Getting them to grasp begging bowls,

This True Love robs sons of Kings!

True Love here is the love of God, and Baba Bulleh Shah describes how it can suddenly enter your heart, clearing doubts and causing an epiphany so that all truth is laid clearly before you.

The first verse perhaps alludes to his first meeting with his future Murshid, Shah Innayat, in Shalimar Gardens in Lahore where teacher and pupil recognised the greatness in the other in the meeting of an eye. With this meeting, Baba Bulleh Shah lost all his senses and everything he had been taught, and gave himself to following his master.

Baba Bulleh Shah says that worldly robbery is different in the sense that people declare others their enemies and then feel justified to attack them and rob them. This can be seen how powerful countries behave before invading others to steal their resources. It can also be seen in the way some people are demonised in society as outsiders or different so that they can be attacked and persecuted. But True Love robs people in a different way by making friends with others and showing kindness and humanity.

In the second verse Baba Bulleh Shah explains that there is no rhyme or reason as to how True Love takes you. It is an inner feeling that comes over you and cannot be controlled and explaining it in scientific terms is no use. It can affect anyone, rich or poor, weak or powerful. Baba Bulleh Shah uses example here of Princes who on experiencing this love, suddenly decide to give up their royal lifestyle and take on a life of wandering, looking for the truth. Siddhartha Gautam who was a prince but became a wanderer looking for God and became the Buddha would have been well known as an example.

"Kassay", plural for "Kassa" means begging bowl (Kashkol) that yogis and wandering holy men carried for offerings of food made by people.

## 40. Ram, Raheem and Maula (Ram, Raheem tay Maula).

If you have truly understood, then what's this commotion?

What then is this Ram, Raheem and Maula?

I thought this was a good couplet to end this book with as it encompasses everything that Baba Bulleh Shah believed in.

Ram (Rama) is worshipped in Hinduism as the seventh incarnation (Avatar) of Vishnu, who together with Brahma and Shiva, forms the holy trinity (Trimurty) of supreme gods. The three have assigned roles, so that Brahma is the creator of the universe and Shiva the destroyer. Vishnu, in the middle is the preserver and is believed to incarnate on earth in different forms, at different times, to redress the balance between good and evil. As such, his seventh incarnation in the form of Rama is particularly significant and is immortalised in the epic Hindu poem Ramayana.

A major section of Hindus believe that Vishnu is in fact the one and only God, who incarnates in different forms so that Rama was a manifestation of this one true god. This form of Hindu monotheism is called Vaishnavism and has many parallels with other monotheistic religions including Islam, Sikhi and Buddhism.

"Maula" is an Arabic word that has multiple meanings and in Punjabi refers to a lord or master or any powerful benefactor. At times when people did not own land but worked for others as serfs (mazzaray), the powerful landowner would be addressed as "Maula". God being the ultimate, powerful Lord and Master is hence also referred to as "Maula" in Punjabi.

"Al-Raheem" is one of the ninety-nine names used by Muslims for God, meaning "All Merciful". This title for Allah conveys His love and compassion for His creation, kindling the hope that He will overlook our sins and forgive us.

In this powerful couplet, Baba Bulleh Shah addresses the three communities of Hindus, Muslims and Sikhs, and points out that they all worship the same One True God, only the mode of worship is different. But when you look at the message each religion attributes to God, there is no difference between the three. So, if each community truly understands the message of their deity, they would know that the message is the same in each one. Once this is understood, none of the differences between faiths matter as we all worship the same One God. In effect he is encouraging people to overlook their differences, stop violence against each other and live in harmony.

## About the Author

Dr. Wasim Ahmed was born in Jammu and Kashmir and came to the United Kingdom as a child, where he has lived ever since. Determined to study medicine, he qualified as a doctor from Imperial College London and subsequently trained as a general practitioner. He has worked in the National Health Service most of his life.

Growing up in the UK, Dr. Ahmed never forgot his Punjabi and Urdu mother-tongues and is proud of his South Asian culture and heritage. He has always been interested in Sufi poetry and is keen to preserve and promote it by translation into English.

Dr. Ahmed particularly admires the work of Baba Bulleh Shah and published his first book, 'Baba Bulleh Shah, A selection of his Punjabi poetry' in 2024.

World history, especially South Asian, colonial and Islamic history are of great interest to Dr. Ahmed. He has travelled widely and loves getting to know about different languages and cultures.

Dr. Ahmed lives in London and spends his spare time reading, writing and nurturing plants in his small garden.